D1285835

DISCARD

Wakarusa Public Library

LEADING WOMEN

Megyn Kelly

From Lawyer
to Prime-Time
Anchor

PHOEBE COLLINS

Cavendish
Square

New York

Published in 2018 by Cavendish Square Publishing, LLC
243 5th Avenue, Suite 136, New York, NY 10016

Copyright © 2018 by Cavendish Square Publishing, LLC

First Edition

No part of this publication may be reproduced, stored in a retrieval system, or transmitted in any form or by any means—electronic, mechanical, photocopying, recording, or otherwise—without the prior permission of the copyright owner. Request for permission should be addressed to Permissions, Cavendish Square Publishing, 243 5th Avenue, Suite 136, New York, NY 10016. Tel (877) 980-4450; fax (877) 980-4454.

Website: cavendishsq.com

This publication represents the opinions and views of the author based on his or her personal experience, knowledge, and research. The information in this book serves as a general guide only. The author and publisher have used their best efforts in preparing this book and disclaim liability rising directly or indirectly from the use and application of this book.

All websites were available and accurate when this book was sent to press.

Library of Congress Cataloging-in-Publication Data

Names: Collins, Phoebe author.
Title: Megyn Kelly : from lawyer to prime-time anchor / Phoebe Collins.
Description: New York : Cavendish Square Publishing, 2018. | Series: Leading women | Includes bibliographical references and index.
Identifiers: LCCN 2017015455 (print) | LCCN 2017033043 (ebook) | ISBN 9781502631794 (E-book) | ISBN 9781502631787 (library bound) | ISBN 9781502634092 (pbk.)
Subjects: LCSH: Kelly, Megyn--Juvenile literature. | Women television journalists--United States--Biography. | Television news anchors--United States--Biography.
Classification: LCC PN1992.4.K4255 (ebook) | LCC PN1992.4.K4255 C55 2018 (print) | DDC 070.92 [B] --dc23
LC record available at https://lccn.loc.gov/2017015455

The photographs in this book are used by permission and through the courtesy of: Cover, Neilson Barnard/Getty Images/Hollywood Reporter; p. 1, 46 Jesse Dittmar/The Washington Post/Getty Images; p. 4 Richard Drew/AP Images; p. 7 Seth Poppel Yearbook Library; p. 16 Matt Gagnon/ File: MegynKelly.jpg/Wikimedia Commons; p. 20 ZeWrestler, own work/File: Newhouse Communications Center III, Syracuse University.JPG/Wikimedia Commons; p. 25 Albany Law School/File: Albany Law Reviews.jpg/Wikimedia Commons; p. 27 Albany Law School, own work/ File: Albany Law School.jpg/Wikimedia Commons; p. 30 Gavin Hellier/Photographer's Choice/ Getty Images; p. 34 Wally Gobetz (http://www.flickr.com/photos/wallyg/)/File: September 11 2001 just collapsed.jpg/Wikimedia Commons; p. 36 S Granitz/WireImage/Getty Images; p. 41 WJLA/ http://www.wjla.com/(http://www.wjla.com/advertising/WJLA-NC8-TBD_Credit_App_with_ Standard_Terms_Revised_110410.pdf)/File: Logo of News Channel 8.svg/Wikimedia Commons; p. 43 Jon Kopaloff/FilmMagic/Getty Images; p. 51 Paul Morigi/WireImage/Getty Images; p. 53 Craig Barritt/Getty Images for Cosmopolitan Magazine and WME Live; p. 60 Andy Kropa/Getty Images; p. 63 Catrina Genovese/WireImage/Getty Images; p. 68 Timothy Hiatt/Getty Images; p. 73 Brendan McDermid/Reuters/Alamy Stock Photo; p. 76 D Dipasupil/FilmMagic/Getty Images; p. 85 Bill Clark/CQ Roll Call/Getty Images; p. 89 Ovidiu Hrubar/Shutterstock.com.

Printed in the United States of America

CONTENTS

CHAPTER ONE

Humble Beginnings

T he renowned television anchorwoman Megyn Kelly has a new Manhattan office. Set in the legendary "30 Rock" building, it is just a few blocks yet a world away from the generic skyscraper that houses the Fox News global headquarters. Kelly's announcement of her defection from Fox to NBC, on January 3, 2017, astonished the world of network and cable television. Fox News colleague Howard Kurtz reported on her difficult choice to leave the network:

Megyn Kelly has anchored many news programs with interviews, late-breaking news, and investigative reports.

At the close of Tuesday's "Kelly File," Kelly said she felt a "human connection" to her viewers and also treasures that "particularly when it comes to my children, who are 7, 5 and 3," signaling that her nighttime schedule was a key factor in her decision.

"I have grown up here and been given every chance a young reporter could ever ask for," she said, praising Rupert Murdoch's family for its kindness toward her.[1]

She'd made her name at Fox in her twelve years there. She'd been co-anchor of *America's Newsroom* in 2006. She also anchored *America Live* in 2010 and *The Kelly File* in 2013—the latter becoming one of the highest-rated cable news programs. But suddenly, her image changed. She rocked the boat with accusations of sexual harassment against Fox chairman and CEO Roger Ailes and her labeling of Donald Trump as "dangerous." She had veered in a new direction without warning. The public wanted to know why she was deserting the Fox ship, and for less money at that. The time had come for the seemingly charmed Megyn Kelly to raise the curtain on her past.

Early Beginnings

Megyn Kelly, though born in Champaign, Illinois, on November 18, 1970, soon moved with her family back to their hometown of Syracuse a mere seven months later. The city of Syracuse, located in central New York State, is best known as the host of New York's annual state

Megyn Kelly was a 1988 graduate from Bethlehem Central High School in Delmar, New York.

fair and as the home of the prestigious Syracuse University. Upstate New York would remain forever the Kelly family home. Her early years were spent in the Syracuse suburb of DeWitt, New York. Bisected by the historic Erie Canal, DeWitt is a typical American small town. Megyn was the youngest of three boisterous children—sister Suzanne and brother Pete—with parents Edward and Linda Kelly heading the household.

Kelly's parents maintained that a person's accomplishments were important. Lavish compliments and adulation were in short supply at the Kelly house. No trophies for showing up on time, or money paid for good grades. Instead, they sought to instill a solid work ethic and doctrine of self-reliance in their children. When Suzanne, Pete, or Megyn messed up, they had to find their own way out of trouble. Getting themselves back on track was done without parental intervention. But there was a lighter side, too—dancing and music were always encouraged. Kelly fondly remembers, "My parents let my whole self shine."[2]

On the surface, they were a typical middle-class American family. Dad Ed was a professor of education, while mother Linda (née DeMaio), was an outspoken homemaker. She also worked outside the home as a nurse. Though occasionally combustible, this union of Irish husband and Italian wife proved cheerfully unconventional. Most important, they were happy. After all, their courtship had begun at Greenwich Village's legendary White Horse Tavern, a favorite hangout of bohemian writers and artists. No generic "Brady Bunch," the lively Kelly family lived by their own rules. With parents who came of age in the 1960s, this influence was marked by orange shag carpets and Don McLean blaring "Bye Bye, Miss American Pie" on the stereo. Kelly was free to dance to her heart's content.

But the Kelly home was no hippie commune. Devout Catholics, the family was firm in their respect for tradition. Yet while proper behavior was always expected, there was still room for plenty of self-expression. Kelly has affectionate memories of her father's constant and kindly encouragement, and of learning (sometimes the hard way) how to successfully defend herself against schoolyard brats. No crying or running for help. Indeed, self-sufficiency, Kelly readily acknowledges, was in her DNA. Neither parent ever backed down from a challenge. "My mother managed a lot back then, and even today I'm not quite sure how. She was working as a nurse and studying for her PhD and raising three kids … My mom worked very hard, and she was my role model."[3]

That Kelly enjoyed such inspiring examples in both her parents is not surprising. They worked hard while sensibly prioritizing their relationships. They raised three fine children, and still made time for fun. They attended church every Sunday and lived by the Bible's moral teachings. This showed in their consideration toward others and love for their neighbors. They practiced random acts of kindness. Pride was never allowed to prevent a healing moment. Conflicts were dealt with quickly, fairly, and often downright humorously. Kelly remembers the time her laid-back father ended an argument with mom Linda. Slowly pouring the contents of his cocktail glass over his wife's head, he then gently massaged it through her hair. As usual in the Kelly home, irritation quickly dissolved into laughter.

With the family unable to afford expensive vacations, Kelly also learned how to make do with anything at hand. She targeted what was nearby. She took charge in developing her intellectual curiosity, courage, and resourcefulness. As anyone who's been there knows, central New York State is a wonderful area for all kinds of day trips. The Kelly family favorite, Selkirk Shores State Park on the shores of Lake Ontario, was an easy drive. The region also features historic villages such as Cazenovia, Skaneateles, and Cooperstown, home of the Baseball Hall of Fame.

Another important female influence in Kelly's life has been her beloved, freewheeling maternal grandmother, Antoinette Frances Holzworth DeMaio. Called "Nana" by her grandchildren, she was a product of the **Depression** years. Nana had been forced to drop out of high school in order to work at the Comfort Coal Factory, where her father labored as a menial shoveler. Eventually, she wound up working for the phone company (or "Ma Bell" as it was called in the old days). She had to abandon her dream of becoming a nurse. No money meant no school. Eventually, she married and raised a family. Some fifty years later, her granddaughter Megyn took up the cause of her grandmother's lost education. Penning a letter to Nana's alma mater, Park Ridge High School in New Jersey, she related the story. She also requested an honorary diploma for her family matriarch. It took some time for the school to track down Nana's records, but in the end, they did. Nana finally graduated with the class of 1997, dressed for the occasion in her favorite flowered dress, a special corsage, and sneakers on her feet. She was the ultimate nontraditional student in a sea of mortarboards and robes. Hers was the broadest smile on the stage. It would not be the first time Kelly stepped up to the plate to help others.

Kelly had no illusions about an easy life, not for her— an average young girl without wealth or connections. The message rang out loud and clear from various sources. Her parents and Nana were people who'd worked their way up. Only hard work, persistence, honesty, and faith would pave the way. But it didn't mean life was grim. Humor and fun were an integral part of the plan, too, along with dancing at every opportunity.

Challenges in a New Town

In 1980, the Kelly family moved 145 miles (233 kilometers) east of DeWitt to Delmar, close to Albany, New York. Transitioning easily to the new town and school, Kelly fit in well and enjoyed her fifth-grade classes. Social life, however, overshadowed academics, where, at this point, she was happy to coast. The next few years brought the commonplace woes of early adolescence—acne, excess weight, and crooked teeth. A close friend urged her not to worry, that Farrah Fawcett had been an "ugly duckling," too. Rather than feeling offended, Kelly felt encouraged. She always looked on the bright side.

And then, it happened. Seventh grade. One of the bland years marking the divide between elementary and high school. Kelly remembers it vividly. Even now, as a world-famous journalist, the memory still haunts her. It was a year marked by betrayal and bullying, and by sudden ostracizing. Also known as the silent treatment, "ostracizing" is defined by the Oxford English Dictionary as "banishment from a society or group." Indeed, it's no coincidence that the harshest punishment in prison is the dreaded solitary confinement. Once surrounded by a congenial social circle, Kelly became isolated. Gradually taking a more aggressive form, this cruel behavior evolved into schoolmates (or the "Group" as she came to think of them) becoming meaner. They tripped Kelly in the hallway, threw spitballs into her hair, laughed at her clothes, and made crude comments about her appearance. Kelly aptly terms it "the total elimination of me as a person."[4]

Another painful aspect of this experience was shame. What, Kelly wondered, had she done to deserve such cruelty? Unsurprisingly, Kelly's natural self-confidence dropped in proportion to her rising self-blame.

The psychological stress was agonizing. At that time, she had no extracurricular activities or hobbies to provide other social outlets. After school, she sat alone at home and self-medicated with food. Worse yet, when she finally reached out for help to the school guidance counselor, he dismissed her complaints. Back then, bullying was not recognized as the serious crisis that it is today. Now, talk shows abound with guests recounting their own stories of suffering, and Amazon offers hundreds of books on the subject. A week doesn't seem to pass without a tragic news story of a child driven to suicide by relentless bullying. Strangely, it is worse now, thanks to social media, cell phones, and the internet. At least back in the 1980s, venues for bullies were fewer and more straightforward. On the other hand, a conspiracy of silence often protected such people. Not anymore. Such behavior can be quickly publicized, and the perpetrators identified.

Back in the 1980s, such was not the case. One terrible night, the phone rang. It was one of the Group. For a moment, her hopes soared. She was asked if she knew where all the kids from the party were. When Kelly responded with a no, they all shouted in unison, "We're here!" and hung up. That was it. She fled to the snow-covered backyard as tears soaked her face. "Raw, terrible pain" are the words Kelly still uses to describe that night.[5] It's easy to wonder why she didn't confide in her supportive mother. But Kelly feared, as so many abuse victims do, of making the situation worse by blowing the whistle. It seemed the lesser of two evils to suffer silently than go public.

A Light at the End of the Tunnel

Finally, the weather broke. A miracle occurred. A morally courageous girl named Heather Shepherd, unconcerned about her own social standing, befriended the depressed Kelly. All it took was a simple "hi." They took to having lunch together, and little by little, Kelly began to feel better. On top of that, the entire Group ended their bullying as suddenly as they had started. Relief was all she felt when it was over.

Kelly encountered these same schoolmates at a reunion years later, after she had become famous. She was the glamorous star of Fox News and recent inductee into the school's Hall of Fame. It hit her that she was, in a way, two people: the Megyn before bullying, and

Reaching Out to Others

Megyn Kelly feels strongly about sharing her experiences. She speaks openly about her own childhood bullying. This is the way to help other victims. Recalling the group of vicious twelve-year-old girls who made her life miserable, she has a surprising view of it today. Her youthful resolve to be tough and indestructible made sense at the time. It was a good survival strategy for school. It was pretty good for law school and her corporate law career. But it did not stand the test of time. "Killer litigation" ability did not translate to television.

Bravado was one thing, but complete lack of openness was another. Kelly learned this when she was starting out on Fox News. No one knew who she really was. Her Fox News mentor Brit Hume expressed his view that "zero vulnerability" made for a one-dimensional broadcaster.[6] Kelly took it to heart, and her life changed. Out with her façade of "fake perfection." The results were wonderful. Personal relationships deepened. Life got better. Overcoming her fear, her natural warmth and humanity emerged on-screen. In equal measure, her inner anger dissipated and there were fewer conflicts with coworkers. This big change was empowered by Kelly's brave admission: she wasn't perfect.

the Megyn afterward. Thanks to the values instilled by her family and church, the bitter experience had not hardened her heart. Rather, it had made her a more compassionate person. The type of person whose strong feelings are leavened with sensitive insights and moral balance. The type of person who makes a great interviewer. And the type of person who, when the time comes, has the guts to blow the whistle on anyone, no matter how powerful they are.

Nevertheless, Kelly is honest enough to say that part of her, as a result of the bullying episode, long maintained an "interior wall" as a means of self-protection—a safe room of sorts, ensuring that no one could see her vulnerability or get close enough to hurt her. Luckily, she is past it now. She is able to be who she is, openly and without fear. She understands that, in life, while it is impossible to avoid cruelty, it doesn't last forever. She no longer hesitates to speak up in the face of injustice. "To this day," she says, "I can handle people who are dumb, lazy, or generally annoying. The one thing I cannot and will not tolerate is a bully."[7]

CHAPTER TWO

Early Successes

After middle school, Bethlehem Central High School provided a broader arena for Kelly. Excelling in sports, she was also captain of the cheerleading squad and homecoming princess. With orthodontist-fixed teeth and a significant weight loss due to her newfound love of running, the so-called "ugly duckling" was blossoming into a swan.

Tragedy Strikes the Kellys

Kelly's high school years were mostly happy, punctuated by the usual teenaged hijinks. A certain shoplifting caper led to an embarrassed apology to the local K-Mart

Megyn Kelly reports from the floor of the 2012 Republican Convention in Tampa, Florida.

manager while returning some pinched jewelry. However, a tragedy during her sophomore year would change her life forever. Ten days before Christmas 1985, Kelly uncharacteristically got into a fight with her usually mild-mannered father. She badly wanted a pricey class ring. All the other girls had them. "Too expensive," he insisted. "We [can't] afford it."[1] Those would turn out to be the last words he ever spoke to his youngest child.

As the conflict escalated, her father abruptly left the kitchen. Kelly stomped off to her own room to sulk. Sleep had overtaken her when suddenly it was midnight, and her sister, Suzanne, was frantically shaking her awake. Her dad had just had a heart attack. For the rest of her life, even if she lives as long as her hundred-year-old Nana, Kelly knows she'll be haunted by her last sight of her dear father, slumped into a chair. Alone, he was still aggravated due to her petty behavior and just stared blankly at the Christmas tree.

As so often happens in grave emergencies, time slid sideways and it seemed like everything was moving in slow motion. Not long afterward, Ed Kelly's wife, two daughters, and son were in the hospital waiting room. They heard a doctor's grim news, "Nothing they could do." After a few minutes of stunned silence, they entered his room together and said good-bye to the husband and father they loved so much.

Years later, Kelly learned to cope with any lingering guilt about the night of her father's death. Pain is never healed entirely, but life does go on. As she herself put it, "The test of strength is not avoiding emotional distress; it's functioning in the face of it."[2] In other words, when you're going through challenges, keep right on going.

But for now, real financial hardship threatened the family. There was a recently canceled life insurance policy and newly purchased car. No longer lively and boisterous, Linda Kelly would arrive home from work and have a good cry before composing herself to face her kids. They were not fooled. Trying to return the car for a much-needed refund, all she got was cold refusal from an intimidating car dealership executive. She then consulted their family lawyer. This well-educated, cultured gentleman composed a pithy and unhelpful letter to the heartless car dealership. Reading it, something clicked within the grieving Megyn Kelly. There could be another, more civilized way of taking bullies down. It was called the law. Like the Kelly family, it was strict and controlled but contained within it endless opportunities for wit and humor. It remained ever **stalwart** in the pursuit of justice.

College and Law School

After her 1988 high school graduation, Kelly started college at the top-ranked Syracuse University. While thrilled to be accepted at SU, being turned down for her first choice, the school's S. I. Newhouse School of Public Communications, was a tough break. Though disappointed, she took it in stride. She instead majored

Syracuse University's S. I. Newhouse School of Public Communications

in political science and completed her bachelor's degree in 1992. Kelly moved from strength to strength. She supported her academic workload with waitressing jobs. She attended sports events and began to enjoy meaningful friendships. On January 26, 1991, she confided to her journal:

> I am twenty years old now and have actively begun to make what I want happen. It's a good feeling, though certainly frightening. I know who I am becoming and who I want to be. The horrifying threat of misplaced nostalgia will never affect me as I age, for—succeed or fail—I will have accomplished the satisfaction of attempting.[3]

Kelly's natural affinity for debate and argument began to flourish, too. After graduation, it was a natural progression to law school. Undeterred by her rejection from the University of Notre Dame, she made second choice her first choice. This meant heading straight to the Albany Law School. There, she edited the *Albany Law Review* and served on a panel that heard sexual harassment complaints against faculty—prophetic in hindsight. At the time, however, it was but one more impressive feather in her cap. Not only attractive but smart, Kelly was susceptible to jealousy from other students, some of whom took to calling her "Barbie." She didn't let it get her down. Just as when she was compared to "ugly duckling" Farrah Fawcett, Kelly looked at the bright side. She had hit her stride and was thriving, with fine grades to show for it. Although she loved her coursework, her sights had now been raised toward a major goal: moot court. This is a mock court at which law students argue imaginary cases for practice. In this way, they gain invaluable experience. Moot court experience upgrades their transcripts for future job searches. And moot court participants enjoy the advantage of intensive training in important areas. Their oral and written **appellate** skills (where decisions are reversed), trial advocacy, and client counseling and negotiation abilities improve markedly.

First-year law students could not try out for moot court; they had to wait until their second year. Ultimately, the teams were made up mostly of third-year students. Throughout her first year, Kelly stayed shrewdly abreast of all moot court activity. She studiously familiarized herself with every aspect of its demands. It wasn't about being witty or entertaining to engage an audience. It was about presenting riveting, no-nonsense arguments to win cases. It was about defeating an opponent. Kelly believed herself equal to the task. After all, public speaking had been a favorite course in high school. Not only that, but she'd excelled at a summer job as a telemarketer. Her voice, she'd been told, had a quality rare in one so young: authority. She knew how to make people listen. Thus, in the years preceding moot court, she fine-tuned her instrument. Tone, shading, inflection, and the strategic use of pauses, already second nature, improved markedly. The more she practiced, the better she got. Her vocal gifts and poise added compelling depth to an intellect firmly grounded in the principles of legal argument. This, she realized, was a powerful secret weapon.

When the big moment arrived, she was ready. Before her tryout, she had spent weeks preparing the prosecution argument for a fictional rape case. During long nights of meticulously crafting her argument section by section, she practiced in front of any makeshift audience—fellow students, the mirror, anything. She learned her closing argument backward and forward, independent of notes. It was wonderful to discover her talent for memorization.

Also attending the moot court tryout that day was an unexpected observer, the legendary criminal procedure professor Ken Melilli. A graduate of Yale and New York

Universities, he had served with distinction as a **federal prosecutor** before returning to academia. He was now a much-admired professor as well as head trial team coach.

From the moment Kelly began, her adrenaline took over. As with elite athletes and great performers, all external distractions vanished. She controlled her **rhetoric** the way Jeff Gordon maneuvers a converted Dodge at top speed on the NASCAR track. She later found out that Melilli and his assistant coach were so impressed that they enthusiastically high-fived each other after she left the room. For Kelly, this was more than just another academic success. This was the pivotal moment that would change the trajectory of her life. There was no need for the trust fund or powerful connections that grease the wheels for so many others. Her instincts about her abilities had proven true. She was indeed far more than a "cheerleader who could type fast," let alone a "Barbie."

However, Kelly's law school days were not without their disappointments, too. At the close of her first year at Albany Law, she wasn't chosen to "grade on" to the prestigious *Albany Law Review.* This meant being in the top 10 percent of the class. It was a critical résumé builder for any law student. The disappointment was terrible. But it wasn't the end, not for Megyn Kelly.

Boldly, Kelly spent the next month studying night and day to be one of the favored few who, as a member of the top 20 percent of her class, could attempt to "write on" to the *Law Review* instead. All the while, she was teaching aerobics classes on weekends and clerking at a Syracuse law firm. This hectic work schedule foreshadowed her future life in corporate law and television. Though tough, it provided the foundation for the greater demands and challenges she was to face. It served her well.

The Syracuse firm provided one unpleasant, though realistic, learning experience. After working hard with the senior law firm partner on a particularly depressing drunk-driving case, he one day called her into his office. He did not applaud her work; he only wanted to know if she'd be interested in meeting his son. He was checking to see, it seemed, if she'd prefer life as a future daughter-in-law rather than a future associate. It did not upset her terribly. That senior partner was from another generation. Even so, the message was clear: her work would be judged differently from that of her male colleagues. She tucked that particular message away for future reference and carried on with academia.

Soon she triumphed on her "write on" project for the *Law Review*. Recalls Michael Hutter, one of her law school professors, "She was an absolutely terrific student, thoughtful ... I always thought she was going to be the next great female trial lawyer in the United States."[4]

Kelly did indeed embrace her moot court experience. She won Best Individual Advocate, scoring the highest marks ever received in the competition. Her team also came in second. But, to use one of her favorite expressions, she "never got too drunk on [her] own wine."[5] The best advice she ever heard regarding humility came from a past Albany Law professor, Ken Melilli, the one who attended her moot court triumph. She calls it her "Albany Law School Theory of Life." His words were these: "Look, for those of you sitting here feeling bad about yourself because you're in danger of failing out, don't beat yourself up too badly. Just remember, you're still in law school—something thousands of others wanted but were denied. And for those of you at the top of your class, feeling great about yourselves and thinking, 'I've got it made,' just remember: you're still at Albany."[6] For Kelly, that meant, "However low you are, there is always something to feel proud of, and however high you are, there is always something to humble you." Kelly affirms, "I hold on to that to this day. My mother is only too happy to help."[7]

Entering Adult Life

Still, there were failures to be overcome. She was turned down by the first law firm she applied to—the same one in Syracuse where she'd clerked. This was an especially bitter blow, since students were expected to get job offers from the firms where they had done such work. But instead, they told her they didn't have the budget to take her on. It seemed to destroy the growing momentum she had built throughout law school. She also felt humiliated in front of her fellow students. This caused her to invent a story about turning down the firm's offer. It meant staying in Syracuse, she said, which she didn't want to do.

Unused to such rejection, especially when she believed herself to be doing great work, Kelly took stock. She feared that if a small Syracuse firm had turned her down, what chances could there be in the major cities? The rejection also felt personal. These despairing thoughts led to a rigid decision. The only way to success would be to cut out all social and fun activities. She would "sacrifice [herself] on the altar of the law."[8] This credo upheld the confident, cool façade necessary to finish up at the law firm. She soldiered through the rest of her time there with a smile on her face and a pleasant attitude. Part of this performance was inspired by her fear of burning bridges. Most important, she would look back in the future and see that this determination to keep showing up, despite failure and humiliation, was invaluable. Many a future work challenge would be conquered by her ability to ignore emotions and plunge into the job at hand.

Graduating from Albany Law School with honors in 1995, Kelly headed toward the notoriously cutthroat world of corporate law. She successfully landed an associate position at the Chicago office of the aggressive Dallas-based firm of Bickel and Brewer, known both for its "Rambo litigation" and for hiring third-year law students at generous Manhattan salaries. Yet again, rejection from her first-choice Syracuse firm opened

Megyn Kelly graduated with honors from the distinguished Albany Law School in 1995.

the door to a far better opportunity. After suffering the unexpected death of her father, Kelly had worked her way through both college and law school, making do on a shoestring budget. She wound up with $100,000 in student debt and a disconnected phone. Understandably, at this point in her life, financial prosperity was her main goal. Getting hired at Bickel, and against major Ivy League competition at that, was akin to winning the lottery. Her lifestyle improved rapidly with an $85,000 starting salary—far more, needless to say, than she'd made teaching aerobics.

Career Girl in a Man's World

Though willing to tolerate Bickel and Brewer's dress code of skirts, rather than pants, for women employees, she pushed back on something else. This was the issue of a junior associate doing the photocopying—a job for support staff. For one thing, it was dishonest to charge clients lawyer fees for menial tasks. While gender issues had never especially bothered Kelly, this was different. As the sole female constantly expected to run the Xerox, her pride, not to mention her ethical code, kicked in.

Confronting her boss directly, she asked him a bold question: Did firm partner John Bickel do his own copying? It did the trick. With that, her copying days were finished. She also gained an important insight: placing principles over paycheck was fine. First, though, you have to make yourself indispensable. You have to build up such a stellar reputation that your professional safety net is firmly in place. Another job would always be on the horizon for so valuable an employee. Experiences such as this would teach Megyn Kelly how to become a powerful advocate and role model for working women.

At Bickel and Brewer, her dogged personality and patient, scrupulous research skills, along with a sharp understanding of **jurisdictional rules** and legal **nuances**, kept her professionally fulfilled. Life in the big city of Chicago was a revelation. Shops, restaurants, theaters, social activities of all kinds, and the vast beauty of Lake Michigan were at her doorstep—not that her brutal work schedule allowed time to enjoy them. Though she was the only female attorney in the Chicago office, her male colleagues soon grew to respect her. They admired her no-nonsense attitude and refreshing lack of prudishness regarding salty language and the inevitable locker-room talk that sometimes rocked the conference rooms during tense strategy sessions. She wasn't the daughter of blunt Linda DeMaio Kelly and granddaughter of the tough, Depression survivor Nana DeMaio for nothing.

CHAPTER THREE

Entry into the Public Eye

L ife in the big leagues of corporate law was as exciting as Bickel and Brewer had promised. But it wasn't personally fulfilling. As the years passed, Kelly gradually began to feel discontented. The manic workload typical to a high-powered corporate firm left no time for the social and leisure activities necessary to lead a balanced life.

Bright Lights, Big City

Then she remembered she had a favorite law school professor associated with the globally renowned Jones Day firm. The connection clicked. Many phone calls,

Chicago is where Kelly got her professional start in corporate law.

emails, and a few anxious days later, she was on a plane to New York to meet in person at their Financial District office. The change felt exhilarating. Though still in the same profession, she'd be in a different urban landscape, one with new people and challenges of all kinds. Her mind was made up by the time she stepped back out onto Vesey Street, close to the World Trade Center. She knew in her heart the interview had been successful. Jones Day would now be home.

Packing up to move from Chicago to New York was no problem. Saying good-bye to someone who had become special was. Dan Kendall was a medical student she'd met in August of 1997, and they were at a point in their relationship where marriage was on the table. Agreeing on a long-distance relationship, Kelly moved to New York at summer's end. They both accepted that their careers in law and medicine were demanding fields. Each required fluidity and tolerance in a couple. Initially daunted by the reality of New York City, Kelly was repelled by its rather filthy subway system. Being the new kid on the block and having to prove herself all over again felt like too much. Boisterous New Yorkers seemed rude after the quiet, friendly midwesterners she was used to. Uncharacteristically, Kelly fell prey to self-pity.

Listening to an extensive litany of complaints over the phone one night, Linda Kelly lost patience with her daughter. Such plain talking worked better than any consoling sympathy. It was the verbal equivalent of a bucket of cold water. Kelly saw immediately that it was time to grow up, stop complaining about trivialities, and count her abundant blessings.

Kendall eventually found a job at a Manhattan hospital. He, too, caught a one-way plane to New York, where he moved in with Kelly for good. She was in love with the man she would marry, and she was earning a fantastic salary at a job she loved. As Kelly says of that time, "If life was a contest, was I ever winning it."[1] And winning was what had driven her for years.

When Kendall transferred to Northwestern University Hospital back in Chicago, Jones Day made room for Kelly at their Chicago office. Soon, Kelly and Kendall were married. Then, at home one early fall morning, she turned on the television news. A major disaster in Manhattan was being reported. It was September 11, 2001. A plane had hit one of the World Trade Center towers. As the words on the crawler spelled out the news across the screen, Kelly's blood froze. She called Kendall in surgery. Then, phone still pressed against her ear and eyes glued to the set, her shock intensified. Another plane, a commercial airliner like the first one, deliberately slammed into the south tower.

She remembered her former apartment house in New York, steps away from the World Trade Center. Faces of colleagues, neighbors, shopkeepers, doormen, and building staff flew through her mind. She saw herself racing down the Vesey Street Stairs. Against all logic, she wanted to be

The September 11, 2001, attacks on the World Trade Center were life-changing for Americans.

back there, not just staring at a television set in Chicago. Something shifted within Kelly. She was a different person from the one who'd first awakened that morning.

The Birth of New Ideas

The next few days of ensuing television news coverage were mesmerizing. Two broadcasters stood out: ABC's urbane Peter Jennings and Ashleigh Banfield of MSNBC. Banfield, out on the street, kept her cool when the World Trade Center crashed down behind her. Always impressed by good reporters, Kelly paid rapt attention as so many familiar faces were transformed by greatness. No panic, just grace and compassion, along with meticulous reportage amid unimaginable chaos. These reporters did more than simply report facts. They were holding their traumatized audience together with sheer professionalism and heroic composure. For the first time in years, she found herself regretting the rejection from the S. I. Newhouse School of Public Communications at Syracuse University. She wasn't alone. September 11, 2001, for many people, was a big wake-up call. A lot of folks took a hard look at their lives and thought about significant changes. So did attorney Megyn Kelly of Jones Day. Immediately, Kelly began to explore her top transferable skills, such as exchanging ideas confidently with powerful people in senior positions, sensing what made them tick, and discovering how best to handle them in different situations.

Enter Oprah and Dr. Phil

Megyn Kelly has always been lucky when it comes to good mentors. After moving back to Chicago, she encountered the most important one of all: Oprah Winfrey. Rather than having a personal meeting with the TV star, Kelly found herself, night after night, sitting raptly before midnight reruns of Winfrey's talk show. "We are all," Winfrey said one night, "one decision away from changing our lives."[2] Kelly sat up a little straighter. Winfrey, she realized, despite her hardscrabble background, "never wallowed in any sort of victimhood … She didn't play the gender card and didn't play the race card. She was just so good we couldn't ignore her."[3]

On another memorable episode, the affable television psychiatrist Dr. Phil put it another way: "The only difference between you and someone you envy is, you settled for less."[4] Kelly was electrified. All the disconnected thoughts floating around in her psyche were suddenly articulated, and they spelled out a clear message: Kelly, rather than having everything, had cheated herself.

Oprah Winfrey at the thirtieth annual People's Choice Awards on January 11, 2004

36

Over her years in law practice, she'd grown a tough hide and a quick wit. She had conquered the impulse to respond emotionally. Instead, she became an expert at staying outwardly calm and turning the tables before an adversary knew what had happened. It made her think of certain broadcasters she admired.

Like a champion tennis player at the net, Kelly had been smashing every ball back, winning points, without considering the entire match as a whole. September 11, 2001, changed all that. Life, she saw, really does hang on a thread. That night she recorded a personal vow in her journal: "I will be out of the law by this time next year."[5]

In the uncompromising pursuit of what the world judges as "success," she had discarded crucial elements of her being. Trust, creativity, adventure, friendship, and time to contemplate life. Important time to think about how to make a difference in the world—this was what mattered, not impressing people with her big paycheck and outwardly flashy lifestyle.

Insights were now flowing rapidly. How could she not have seen the message of her father's early death? Live your own life to the fullest, and don't waste a moment doing otherwise. Hard work, if bereft of meaning, is useless. Then she remembered that favorite song by John Denver she and her father used to sing together:

I can't be contented with yesterday's glory
I can't live on promises, winter to spring
Today is my moment. Now is my story.
I'll laugh, and I'll cry, and I'll sing.[6]

Getting Her Foot in the Door

The time had come to be more specific. What experience did she have to get her hired at any level of the television news industry? So far it was not impressive. A two-day internship as a teenager, amid a field crowded with talented people all reaching for the same brass ring. And her competition was ten years younger, armed with journalism degrees and professional experience.

Slowly, Kelly tested the waters. The initial results of her cold-calling efforts to various television stations were depressing. Rather than give up, she listened to her inner self. She signed up for a guitar class, restoring the beauty of music to her life. The small, creative group of musicians raised her spirits. She learned that a fellow classmate, Meredith, worked as a freelance journalist. An old pro at networking and building fast friendships, the intrepid Kelly took Meredith to a coffee shop and learned as much as she could about local television news. She was especially interested in hiring procedures, the nature of producing broadcasts, and what it would take to get her foot in the door.

What she needed most was a killer audition tape. Meredith, whom Kelly had come to think of as "Saint

Meredith," offered to help her with this momentous project. Cameraman Bond Lee at Chicago's local NBC affiliate (WMAQ-TV) was soon recruited. As a challenge, Lee gave her sixty seconds to dazzle him with a news story. For her story, she chose the upcoming parole of the notorious "preppy murderer," Robert Chambers.

For the next few weeks, she shadowed WMAQ's news team, learning the lingo of the profession and how to fit in. She became an instant location scout, researching special stories for each one. Instead of unrelated details or half-formed ideas, she had the whole picture in focus this time. She could soon skip around within the broadcast story structure without becoming flustered, an essential art for a successful newsperson. She could improvise and think on her feet, without hours of perfectionist rehearsal.

The hardest element, surprisingly, was telling an engaging story in ninety seconds without stumbling over her words or relying on useless conversational crutches such as "um," "uh," or worse yet, "you know." Meanwhile, broadcast television was not a corporate conference room. The kind of support systems Kelly had come to rely on—other people's reactions, strategic body language, or dramatically timed pauses—didn't translate to live television. Just as when Ashleigh Banfield maintained her composure as the World Trade Center crashed down behind her, the story came first, the reporter second. This meant negotiating the delicate balance between projecting a natural charisma that engaged an audience and not distracting from the actual news.

Thanks to Meredith and Bond Lee, a professional audition tape was produced. But just when things were rolling, fate tossed one of its curveballs. Kelly's husband, Dan Kendall, received an offer from the preeminent medical institution Johns Hopkins to do a pain management fellowship. It was time to pull up stakes and move again, this time to Baltimore, Maryland. The worst aspect of this move for Kelly was its disruption of the discreet momentum she was building.

Jones Day again came through, this time with a transfer to their Washington, DC, office, but it in no way compared with her early time at the firm. This was a different Megyn Kelly. Her ambitions were elsewhere, and the world of corporate law was receding into the background. Where she once attacked cases with gusto, she now just went through the motions. In an attempt to bloom where she was planted, Kelly took to scrutinizing the help-wanted advertisements. To her dismay, she found that every television offer insisted on at least three years of news experience.

The competitive Baltimore and Washington television news markets were out of reach for a newcomer. She needed, like many a newscaster before her, a small-town station to get her start. Remembering Dr. Phil's prophetic words about settling for less, she felt even more pessimistic.

Megyn Kelly made her local television news debut in 2003.

One day, another television program opened a new door. This was a Lifetime documentary on the late Jessica Savitch. As the anchor for the weekend editions of NBC's *Nightly News* in the late 1970s through early 1980s, she was one of the first solo female anchors of an evening network show—a pioneer in her field. Kelly related powerfully to Savitch's small-town background and snappy appearance. Like her, Savitch had lost her father at a young age. Kelly was especially thrilled to learn that Savitch hit the big time with little professional experience and at the relatively late age of thirty, not twenty-one. Kelly had the uncanny feeling that Savitch was somehow addressing her personally, that she and Savitch were kindred souls of some kind. Once again, a great role model had *found* her. Her conviction renewed, she started yet another round of cold-calling news directors.

Finally, she gained a positive response from the local cable news station, NewsChannel 8. Station manager Bill Lord reluctantly agreed to let the unknown drop off her résumé in person. Quickly doing some research, she was delighted to discover that Lord also ran WJLA-TV, the ABC affiliate. She bought an extravagant Dolce and Gabbana outfit to make the most of this in-person meeting. A résumé, after all, could never convey Kelly's natural charisma, her intelligence, her shrewdness, and her appealing personality. Everything hinged on this first impression—just the sort of challenge Kelly excelled at.

Her choice of Dolce and Gabbana, a luxury Italian fashion house known for cutting-edge, even theatrical, styles, was significant. Years later, a *New York Times* profile on Kelly would draw a connection between her willingness, as an anchor, to challenge prominent guests on the air and her singular fashion sense:

She took on Newt Gingrich over his "anger issues" in October [2016], sparred with the Republican Svengali Karl Rove over his electoral math in 2012 and challenged the conservative radio host Mike Gallagher over his dismissal of maternity leave. These moments have become widely known as "Megyn Moments" ... But what has been less widely acknowledged is that they extend far beyond her reports and interviews at the anchor desk into a broader statement about how women should be able to frame their gender. Put simply, she doesn't just say what she wants. She wears what she wants.[7]

Megyn Kelly looked like a star at *Vanity Fair*'s 2017 Oscar party in Beverly Hills.

"Megyn Moments" rely on the unique intensity that Kelly brings to her interviews, especially when she challenges someone in a position of power. This same intensity and courage is reflected in her wardrobe. Speaking to the *New York Times*, Tammy Haddad, formerly a political director for MSNBC and now the chief executive of Haddad Media, further emphasized the significance of Kelly's wardrobe, saying, "You cannot underestimate the effect of [her clothing choices.] Her personal image and her business image are one and the same. The intensity she brings to her work, she brings to her look … That's good for all women. And it is completely different from what came before."[8]

Leaving Lord's office with a one-day-a-week job that paid a grand total of $176 per day, Kelly was on top of the world. Laughing with her new boss about going from one maligned occupation to another, she inwardly rejoiced. Her dream was starting to happen. While still remaining at Jones Day, her one-day-a-week television job began to expand into additional shifts. It reached a point where she had to ask her mystified boss at the firm for a part-time schedule. Her colleagues were downright bewildered. The head of litigation even made a direct offer of partnership, despite the part-time schedule. But it was too late. A true calling, one that came with the chance to make a difference and be a "somebody" on the world stage, had arrived. There was no turning back now.

Climbing the Television Ladder

Eventually, Lord offered Kelly a full-time television job at WJLA. While some people would have celebrated such a victory, Kelly wasn't sure. Something made her want to aim higher. The confidence boost of Lord's offer provided the courage she needed to roll the dice once more. A few weeks prior, Kelly had met Fox News contributor Bill Sammon at the Television and Radio Correspondents' Association Dinner, an annual event at the Washington Hilton. In the course of their conversation, he encouraged her to contact Kim Hume, Fox's Washington bureau chief and the wife of Brit Hume, who was to play such a crucial role as Kelly's mentor. Sammon suggested that Kelly send an audition tape. Kelly was hesitant, with only eight months of steady television work under her belt. But she kept Sammon's card. A few weeks later, after receiving Bill Lord's offer, she put a call through to Sammon. He supplied Kim Hume's contact information at Fox. If she was good enough for a local job, why not try for a national one? The timing felt right, and it was. The perfect timing, combined with Kelly's dynamic tape and her uncanny intuition, ensured that the stars aligned. Kim Hume was on the phone with Kelly within twenty-four hours of viewing her audition tape. Success was at hand all right, but the storm clouds were forming, temporarily obscured by the sudden limelight.

CHAPTER FOUR

Forging a New Trail

Megyn Kelly's contributions to women in broadcasting, and to working women in general, are manifold. In throwing over a secure job to follow her dream, she created a fresh template for working women of all socioeconomic groups. After a successful law career, she went after national television, and beyond all expectations, she came home with the prize due to diligence and hard work. She then forged a new trail in broadcasting with her winning combination of sharp intelligence, humor, and glamorous good looks for which she made no apology. She called bullying and misogyny by their names. In 2015, after

Megyn Kelly arrived at Fox News in 2004.

eleven years at Fox, her defining moment arrived. In her role as GOP primary debate moderator, she refused to coast over any controversies. Instead, she sent shock waves across the nation by confronting candidate Donald Trump with his own words. No one, male or female, had ever dared to do such a thing at a presidential debate. To put these achievements in perspective, it helps to review the history of women in broadcast journalism.

Women Broadcasters

In 1939, Lowell Thomas (an adventurous early broadcaster famous for his friendship with Lawrence of Arabia) hosted the first television news broadcast. Thirty-seven years later, a woman broadcast journalist finally made it to the same job. Barbara Walters broke the glass ceiling and took the co-anchor's chair in 1976. It heralded a collective step up the ladder for women broadcast journalists. It also announced the dawning of a new era where entertainment, via on-screen personalities, would influence the traditionally austere news business. A public uproar broke out after Walters's promotion. Many felt that she did not support the integrity of the profession as a whole. **Gravitas** was being replaced by a new word, "infotainment," as concern over television ratings brought gossip to the headlines.

Twenty-eight years later, when Megyn Kelly arrived on the scene, women broadcasters were commonplace. Pros like Diane Sawyer, Connie Chung, Katie Couric,

Charlayne Hunter-Gault, and Lesley Stahl were (and are) among the top newswomen in their field. They anchor everything from half-hour nightly network shows to the twenty-four-hour-a-day, seven-day-a-week cable juggernauts that exist today. This new format can be unabashedly **raucous**, courting a "news junkie" audience. Rather than yesteryear's more thoughtful, impartial viewers, this audience wants their own biases (be they left leaning or right) affirmed. Kelly perfectly filled the gap between the two extremes. The time-honored assumption that the Fox News formula worked fine, whoever occupied the anchor chair, was put to the test by Kelly. After all, it was her show that won the number-two ratings spot in cable news—after the rock-solid number-one spot occupied by Bill O'Reilly. (O'Reilly's show, however, was an opinion program, while Kelly's was hard news.) Even a negative, such as Donald Trump's verbal attacks on Kelly, brought more viewers to Fox than the channel had ever known—and not because they agreed with Trump. It was this knowledgeable woman who easily defended herself without playing the victim or dragging politics into it. Her presence at debates and political conventions raised the bar and brought Fox a new gravity. Gone was the old male right-wing cronyism, and in was an intelligent, somewhat unpredictable female voice capable of reaching a wider audience. New demographics such as working women, single mothers, and young people were taking notice. Fox's starchy image began to change for the better.

Learning the Ropes

Working at Fox, as Kelly says, brought a "steep learning curve." But she was a proven hard worker who was adept at picking up new ideas fast. Initially, her shifts began at five in the morning, three days a week, followed by two weekend shifts. The advantage of those off-peak hours was that people tended to be more friendly, relaxed, and off guard. Kelly made the most of this to nurture friendships and better learn the ropes. She found she had to think fast and on her feet. No second tries or extensions were ever offered, as might have been the case in corporate law.

She soon learned how to structure a news story by framing it in a particular context and giving it the right perspective. She continued practicing her reading style and watching playbacks of her tapes. That made it easier to get the jump on any mistakes and catch them before the boss did. Her favorite show was *Special Report with Brit Hume*. Hume supported and guided her, while suffering no nonsense. "It was," Kelly still says, "the best journalistic training ground a young reporter could ask for."[1] It was also imperative to take responsibility for everything that happened on one of her shows. If she couldn't identify a particular sound bite, it wasn't someone else's fault. It was hers.

Power couple Kim and Brit Hume are Kelly's mentors and friends.

Back in 2004, while navigating the landscape of
her new profession, Kelly learned its **idiosyncrasies**
and trade secrets. She came to understand the highly
competitive world of cable news. This should have been
a cakewalk for a woman of her experience. But, as with
all companies, Fox's corporate culture was dictated by its
CEO, and Kelly had never encountered anyone to equal
him. Roger Ailes, the founder and former chairman

and CEO of Fox News and the Fox Television Stations Group, was a force of nature. At age sixty-four, he ruled over the Fox empire like a king. No one talked back to him. No one questioned his dictates—certainly not his newest star, Kelly, who quickly learned to keep her thoughts to herself, at least in his presence.

Meanwhile, her Fox career took off. In time, the segments she either hosted or cohosted included "Kelly's Court" on *Weekend Live*, plus her own weekly segment on *The O'Reilly Factor*, which specialized in law and politics. She often stepped in for regular Fox hosts such as Greta Van Susteren. Growing ever more popular with both the Fox brass and the audience, Kelly successfully anchored many weekend news shows. Viewers especially enjoyed her regular appearances as a guest panelist on Fox's late-night satire program *Red Eye* with Greg Gutfeld.

In 2012, *America Live*, hosted by Kelly, had its highest-rated month ever in total viewers. Furthermore, it enjoyed the second-highest rating in the vital twenty-five to fifty-four age demographic. This achievement meant a lot to Fox because it was eager to shake off its stuffy "old curmudgeon" image. Kelly, with her broad appeal and natural humor, was changing the game. Competing networks took note.

Megyn Kelly cohosted with Kelly Ripa the popular show *Live!* on the morning after Donald Trump's election to the White House in 2016. The ratings for that one show set a record, placing it in the number-one spot for

Megyn Kelly's unique broadcasting style came through when she interviewed Donald Trump.

syndicated programs. It even beat *Dr. Phil* and *Ellen*. Kelly brought Ripa her biggest audience since former cohost Michael Strahan left for *Good Morning America*.

Kelly was a breath of fresh air. She was the catalyst for a new, more inclusive conversation on Fox News programs. She broadened Fox's audience and, in so doing, extended the discourse beyond cable television boundaries. Many women (across the political spectrum) felt empowered to speak up. And most of all, people wanted to know who Kelly was. Many viewers tend to parrot whatever they've heard on the news. Megyn Kelly's goal was to take people beyond their comfort zones and get them looking at themselves, the same way she did. She encouraged them to formulate their own opinions.

The GOP Presidential Primary Debate

The success of her programs showed that Kelly was unique in her contributions and in her professional conduct. Above all, she was her own woman. While she has always behaved with **probity**, she has never been afraid to oppose the **status quo** when necessary. This was confirmed in Cleveland, Ohio, in August 2015, when Kelly moderated the first debate in the Republican presidential primary campaign.

Kelly was earnest about her role as moderator. She had no agenda of her own, other than finding out exactly where each candidate stood on the issues. Along with Fox News colleagues Chris Wallace and Bret Baier, she politely and sincerely questioned the candidates. However, she did not back down when it came to boldly using then-candidate Trump's own language against him. Confronting Trump about his attitude toward women, she explicitly repeated his notorious comments back to him, word for word. The exchange, which had far-reaching ramifications, went like this:

Megyn Who?

When Brit Hume, a senior political analyst for the Fox News channel, first heard about Kelly, he wasn't interested. His wife, Kim, had just brought in some videotape of an unknown, insisting that he view it immediately. Hume was reluctant. A corporate lawyer? New to the business? But after seeing the tape, he changed his mind. He was enthusiastic. As he put it in his statement honoring Kelly as part of the 2014 *Time* 100 list, "Her tape displayed as full a set of the qualities of a network correspondent as I had ever seen: great looks, strong voice, authoritative yet cheerful presence and obvious intelligence. In other words, limitless potential."[2] Not too bad as praise goes, especially from a broadcast legend like Hume.

For Kelly, Hume greatly influenced her journalistic career. The erudite Hume, a respected twenty-three-year news veteran, helped Kelly soften her edges without weakening her performance. He urged her to take full responsibility for all aspects of her work. No blaming cameramen or editors. Most of all, he taught her not to tamper with her special telegenic appeal. The camera loved her; trust it. This freed up her deep-reaching analytical skills and natural humor, to the surprise of many a guest and to the constant delight of her growing audience. Kelly hit it off immediately with both Brit and Kim Hume. They would become close and trusted friends. Like her, they combined courage and intelligence with good humor and an innate toughness.

> *Kelly: You've called women you don't like "fat pigs," "dogs," "slobs," and "disgusting animals." Does that sound to you like the temperament of a man we should elect as president?*
>
> *Trump: What I say is what I say. And honestly, Megyn, if you don't like it, I'm sorry, I've been very nice to you, although I could probably maybe not be, based on the way you have treated me. But I wouldn't do that to you.[3]*

The cross fire caused a sensation that shook the early primaries. Many felt that Kelly had kicked the presumed antifeminist Fox agenda to the curb. It also made Kelly (like Barbara Walters before her at ABC) a break-out personality in the media world. She demanded to be reckoned with.

Megyn Kelly's Broadcasting Influence

Popular with left-of-center viewers as well as the usual conservative Fox audience, the gifted Kelly presented right-leaning stories with humanity and wit. Gone was any rigid self-righteousness or hatred of the other side. The debate exchange was the beginning of a nine-month vendetta, characterized by personal insults and the undermining of her character at every opportunity. Trump also provoked his millions of social media followers to boycott Kelly's show and openly persecute her.

Kelly never forgot her middle school experience of being bullied. Of course, that was minor-league stuff compared to this, but it stood her in good stead. Drawing on her memory of those experiences, Kelly was able to set an example for all women suffering similar workplace degradation. Sexism is sexism, whether it happens behind the counter at a drug store or in the plush environs of the executive suite.

As some Fox News colleagues ostracized her, Kelly serenely kept her cool. She never overreacted or lost her temper, even when it became necessary to engage security guards due to the death threats leveled against her and, later, her family. As Kelly has said, when she and her second husband, Douglas Brunt, took their children to Florida to visit Disney World, an armed security guard accompanied them. His name was Mike, and he'd almost become part of the family.

The bullying continued. At its worst, Trump went so far as to dust off an antiquated nineteenth-century **bromide**—using the menstrual cycle to question a woman's sanity. This refers to a time when Victorian doctors actually believed that women, more so than men, were prone to mental illness due to their monthly cycles. Any vulgarities she'd had to endure during her school days paled in comparison. But this time, it would not be, as in seventh grade, the "total elimination" of her as a person. This was not middle school in a small town. This affected the whole country. Millions of women looked to Megyn Kelly to take a stand for herself and for women everywhere.

In an April 2016 interview with Charlie Rose, Kelly was asked who she thinks her audience is. Kelly said, "The viewer I picture in my mind when I do *The Kelly File* is a woman who's had a long day, either with the kids or at work, or both. She sits down, she gets her glass of chardonnay, she wants to consume the news effortlessly, enjoy it, and not have to work too hard for it."[4]

Sunday Night with Megyn Kelly

Kelly was a high-ranking figure in the 2016 campaign due to her fiery exchanges with Donald Trump. But during the first months of Trump's presidency, Kelly remained in the background, preparing to begin her assignment at NBC News.

On June 4, 2017, *Sunday Night with Megyn Kelly* premiered. While Kelly hoped that *Sunday Night* would distinguish itself from other shows by being innovative and maybe a little rude at times, the premiere seemed very similar to other news shows. In leaving Fox News and launching a show on a new network, Kelly was expected to balance maintaining her identity as a tough interviewer with reinventing herself enough to attract a new audience—one that may expect something different than her fans from Fox.

In the debut episode of *Sunday Night with Megyn Kelly*, there were separate stories from Cynthia

Megyn Kelly interviews Russian president Vladimir Putin on NBC's
Sunday Night with Megyn Kelly.

McFadden and Harry Smith. But the focus of the
debut episode was Kelly's interview with Russian
president Vladimir Putin. The interview took place in
St. Petersburg, Russia. It focused on Russian interference
in the presidential election and Russian cyberespionage.
These topics are particularly challenging and divisive,
which is why there was much hope that Kelly would
bring her characteristically prosecutorial style to the
interview exchange.

Her show received mediocre reviews because
commentators found Kelly's interview questions lacking
in enough substance to really draw out clear answers
from Putin. Putin could evade many questions because

Kelly did not cite specific examples regarding his actions. In the end, the interview was characterized as entertaining rather than newsworthy. Many of her fans still expect to see her strong and unique personality shine through on her new talk show.

Kelly's Morning Show

Even as she launched her new evening show, Kelly was also busy preparing for her NBC morning show, which was set to replace the 9:00 a.m. hour of the *Today* show in the fall of 2017. In the months before the show's premiere, rumors circulated. In April, it was reported that Kelly had interviewed the Kardashian family for the show's first week. In June, it was announced that she had secured Jackie Levin, a longtime *Today* producer, and Katy Davis, a veteran of *The Oprah Winfrey Show*, for her show's production team.

Some commentators expressed concern regarding how Kelly would adjust to daytime broadcasting. Morning audiences tend to want a different style of reporting (some would say "gentler") as compared to evening audiences. The evening audience usually demands the type of reporting—direct and unbiased— that reflects Kelly's style. Other commentators explained that Kelly's background as a lawyer and her role as a mother make her a perfect fit for daytime broadcasting. These experiences make her highly relatable to the typical morning show viewer.

So what do fans ultimately expect when they watch Megyn Kelly? Kelly's fans tune in to see a woman who speaks for them, rather than down to them. They seek a newswoman who performs the investigative **due diligence** herself and who is willing to challenge her guests, whether they be Republicans or Democrats. Indeed, Kelly pokes holes in the doctrine of political correctness with refreshing common sense. She presents her findings with confidence, intelligence, and honesty, and she welcomes audience responses. She relishes her part in energizing the national discourse on significant issues. Thanks in part to Kelly, the role of women on television news has become both more creative and more unorthodox than in Barbara Walters's day.

CHAPTER FIVE

Activism

The Fox News headquarters in New York represented the promised land for many an ambitious dreamer, especially one named Megyn Kelly. It was hard to believe that she got her start in broadcasting as a street reporter for the local Washington, DC, station WJLA. From the day Kelly first came aboard at Fox, however, there was trouble. After all, in a big corporation like Fox, many jobs were at stake. No one, especially a working woman, was willing to speak out and risk her livelihood. Thus, women became the targets and victims of the CEO's sexual harassment. Their male colleagues were safe from such bullying.

The Water Gets Rough

Kelly learned early on about this harassment. According to her, Fox CEO and chairman Roger Ailes hit on her

Megyn Kelly (*right*) poses with fellow Fox News correspondents Kimberly Guilfoyle (*left*) and Jamie Colby (*center*) at the 2015 National Lesbian and Gay Journalists Association benefit in New York City.

when she was new to Fox, back in 2004. He asked lewd questions, and once, he grabbed and kissed her before she broke away and ran. She assumed she was his only target. It was also certainly true that there was another side to him. He could be quite nice. Ailes was good at blurring the lines with **innuendo** and then snapping back to business again, keeping Kelly off guard. She put him off with the usual behavioral strategies. If he propositioned her, she pretended not to hear him, or she pretended that she did not understand what he meant. She kept her distance from him. Ailes was revered as the most powerful man in the industry. Kelly found herself lapsing into typical victim's denial. Maybe his words weren't so bad, she told herself. Perhaps she misunderstood his actions. Who would believe such a story anyway? Then, he threatened her job. As she extricated herself from his grasping arms, he asked, "When is your contract up?"[1] The meaning was clear. As soon as she got home, Kelly telephoned a lawyer friend at Jones Day. He listened sympathetically and noted down all her information.

She decided not to take legal action at that time. Her job at Fox meant the world to her. It was everything she'd dreamed of and worked for. She honestly believed she was alone in it, the only woman that he had bothered. Eventually, Ailes's behavior died down, and in the years that followed, he aged considerably. He wasn't in the office very much, and when he was, he required a walker to get around. During those intervening years, Ailes and

Roger Ailes (*left*) at the Fox News headquarters in 2005

Kelly had actually become friends. She and her husband often dined with Ailes and his wife at their home. Ailes was one of her top fans. Everything was fine. Or was it?

One day, Kelly met another woman at Fox who'd also been harassed by Ailes. Confiding to Kelly that he'd come on to her at her job interview, she also said it never happened again. There and then, Kelly made a promise to herself. "If I heard of him doing this to another woman," she resolved, "I would ... come forward."[2]

Then came Gretchen Carlson's explosive $20 million lawsuit against Ailes for sexual harassment. The popular host of *Fox and Friends* had secretly recorded Ailes's vulgar remarks to her for over a year. With this proof, she went public. Ailes had made the fatal mistake of stereotyping an attractive blond, a former Miss America, no less, as a "bimbo." It backfired badly. She also happened to be a Stanford graduate with a distinguished career in broadcasting.

A host of other coworkers began to confide in Kelly. These were women employees from all areas of Fox News, not just on-air talent. They had little in the way of power and were risking their jobs by speaking up. Inspired by their courage, Kelly took the high road. She told her own story. Their cause was hers.

Thus, she took a stand in solidarity with her Fox women colleagues. The time had come where she could either honor her own integrity or be loyal to Ailes. She could not do both. Formally deposed (interviewed) by the New York law firm of Paul Weiss, Kelly recalled under oath the physical advances and lewd comments she'd endured. Though it had happened long ago, at the beginning of her Fox career, it was crucial evidence. It could save the lower echelon Fox female employees, who stood to lose their jobs for speaking out against injustice. Ailes, as is now common knowledge, was a billionaire abuser and bully who'd been getting away with it for years. Another bitter memory arose, from Kelly's childhood. But she was no longer a defenseless child, far from it.

Instead, Kelly was a powerful celebrity in her own right. And most important, she was a mother. The example owed to her children, especially her daughter, Yardley, took precedence over any other concerns. The unsavory episode finally came to end on July 21, 2016, when Ailes resigned from Fox. But Kelly's personal objectives, as forged in childhood, will never change: to bring down bullies and fight for justice.

Kelly has no illusions that either workplace bullying or sexual harassment has ended. But the Fox women's victory is certainly another nail in the coffin for such behavior. Blaming the victim is no longer tolerated the way it was in the past. Kelly can't help but feel proud to have played a part in that. Additionally, the focus now is increasingly on management, and its responsibility to protect all employees. Significant controls must be in place. All workers must be protected from harassment of any kind. Management is legally bound to respond swiftly to the first signs of a hostile workplace.

The Underdogs' Champion

When an anti–gay marriage activist appeared as a guest on *The Kelly File* in January 2016, he did not receive a warm welcome. National Organization for Marriage president Brian Brown openly expressed strong support for the Alabama State Supreme Court chief justice's order to stop same-sex marriages—even though the Supreme Court of the United States had legalized same-sex marriages across the United States. The Alabama court's order was nothing more than an effort to circumvent the landmark United States Supreme Court ruling in *Obergefell v. Hodges* in June 2015. This ruling made marriage equality the law of the land. Brown apparently forgot that his interviewer was a former attorney. Kelly let him have it with one of her trademark eye rolls followed by a razor-sharp rebuttal. "The Supreme Court has the final say on what the law is!" she exclaimed. "This was established long ago in *Marbury v. Madison*. But here's my question to you … How does this unfold? Aren't we going to have chaos now if states are individually allowed to decide which Supreme Court decisions they're gonna comply with and which they're not?"[3] Most people would have thrown in the towel, but Brown hit back. He dismissed her case citation. He argued that there have always been terrible Supreme

Court decisions that were not constitutional. As he went on in this vein, Kelly's expressive face registered disbelief. Then she rolled her eyes again.

"There's a procedure for that," she deadpanned. "You go back to the legislature and ask them to pass a law." Brown was silent. Before he could say anything more, she smoothly wrapped it up. "Interesting take on it ... Thank you so much for being here. We appreciate it."[4] Same-sex marriage advocates across the country were surprised to find a Fox News reporter standing up for their cause.

Honor Diaries

Honor Diaries is an important documentary film on a terrifying subject. It follows the dialogue between nine brave women's rights advocates with connections to the Muslim-majority societies where gender inequality is a grave problem. Characterizing the abuses permitted in these societies as an international human rights catastrophe, the film gives these suppressed female voices a platform. The reality of genital mutilation is confronted openly, as are forced marriages and educational rights.

One of these women is Ayaan Hirsi Ali, a member of the Dutch parliament from 2003 to 2006. She was born in Somalia and is now a United States citizen. An outspoken defender of Muslim women against Islamist honor violence (the killing of a family member who brought shame to the family), she has suffered genital mutilation. *Honor Diaries* is the first film to speak out

Producer David Coleman speaks at a Chicago screening of *Honor Diaries,* a controversial film on Middle Eastern women's rights.

strongly on so-called honor violence against women and girls. Due to her appearance in the film, and her role as an executive producer of the documentary, she has received death threats. She also helped establish the AHA Foundation, which seeks to protect and defend the rights of women in the West from oppression justified by religion and culture.

A highly controversial figure, Hirsi Ali was no one's first choice as a talk show guest. But Kelly had her on *The Kelly File*, along with Ibrahim Hooper of the Council on American-Islamic Relations (CAIR). The focus of their appearance was Brandeis University's decision to revoke an honorary degree bestowed upon Hirsi Ali. Brandeis had been pressured by CAIR to withdraw the honorary degree, after Hooper termed it "hateful." Ultimately, Brandeis stood by its decision to revoke the award, deciding that Hirsi Ali had upset Muslim students at Brandeis.

However, when Hooper took the stance that Hirsi Ali's allegations of abuse threatened the rights of American Muslims, citing the United States Constitution in his argument, Kelly made no secret of her disgust. Hooper claimed, "Every day we're defending the Constitution from people like Hirsi Ali who would change the Constitution so that Muslims wouldn't have civil rights."[5] Kelly's response was sharp. She cited CAIR's defense of PIJ, a terrorist group that had killed over one hundred people. After a brief but spirited debate on the First Amendment, Kelly ended the discussion. She opined that Hooper's problem was that he would not respond to Hirsi Ali's charges, instead hiding behind silence. It is hard to think of another news program where such a spirited debate would be gracefully moderated without getting out of control. Kelly, as usual, did not shy away from a controversial, even **incendiary**, topic.

How does Kelly do it? For one, she has the ability to show reason and sympathy when faced with nasty, extremist small-mindedness. "There's so much hate for gays and lesbians and transgendered people," she once told a Fox News contributor who was arguing that Cher's son, the transgender Chaz Bono, posed a threat to America. "You seem to be adding to the hate."[6]

Her competition weighs in positively. Famous female journalists from other networks admire her spontaneous charm. "She doesn't talk down to her audience," says Campbell Brown, a former CNN host who now leads an education nonprofit. "There is none of the sanctimonious, condescending attitude. And, frankly, none of the hate. I think people are sick of these prime-time chest thumpers characterizing the other side as evil."[7] Former chief White House correspondent for CNN Jessica Yellin enthuses, "She defies all the pigeonholing that usually happens to women on TV. She's smart, strong, sexy, fierce, sympathetic all at once."[8] Longtime newswoman Katie Couric lauds Kelly's tenacious interviewing aptitude, essential to get under the skin of evasive politicians: "I've noticed that she's a really good listener. Sometimes the tendency is to go down a laundry list of questions and to not say, 'Wait a minute.' It requires you to think on your feet and to take the conversation in a totally different direction."[9]

Black Lives Matter

On April 12, 2015, twenty-five-year-old Freddie Gray, a young black resident of Baltimore, was arrested. According to a court document, Gray had "fled unprovoked upon noticing police presence." Gray "was arrested without force or incident."[10] Then, Gray died in police custody not long afterward. Later, Maryland state prosecutor Marilyn Mosby stated that Gray had been "illegally arrested, assaulted and falsely accused of carrying an illegal switchblade."[11] Upon taking him in, the police had used excessive force. They called the young man "irate" and used this as a reason for their actions. Putting his legs in leg irons and restraining his hands behind his back, they also threw him into the van on his stomach and refused to get the medical help Gray begged for. The case became a nationwide **cause célèbre.**

The public response to this tragedy was swift and retaliatory. It was far from the first time a black suspect had died at the hands of police. While things were quiet for Gray's April 27 funeral, later that same day riots broke out in Baltimore, leaving behind streets filled with debris, burnt or smashed cars, and looted storefronts. All Gray had done, protesters maintained, was run.

Charges were subsequently filed against six Baltimore officers implicated in the arrest and death of Gray. Ultimately, after three of the officers were acquitted, all remaining charges were dropped by prosecutors.

According to the *Baltimore Sun*, this "[brought] to an end one of the highest-profile criminal cases in the city's history with zero convictions."[12] The case may have come to an end, but not the outcry. The organization known as Black Lives Matters was especially outraged, and the case made national news. The entire country was shaken by yet another young African American male fatality. Such incidents were almost becoming commonplace, and many people felt enraged by what they termed "police brutality."

Kelly got involved when *The Kelly File* examined the story. Her guests were prominent attorney Andell Brown, who also happens to be African American, and Milwaukee County Sheriff David Clarke. Kelly's position on the case was, of course, controversial. Although many people disagreed with her, she stuck to her guns and held her own. She refused to get on the bandwagon of police condemnation sweeping the country.

Never one to duck an issue, Kelly got into a heated exchange with Black Lives Matter activist DeRay Mckesson when he appeared on her show. Keeping her questions confined to the letter of the law, she disagreed that police officer Edward Nero's acquittal in the Gray case was, according to a critic, "biased and racist to the core."[13] When Mckesson retorted that laws needed to be in place to hold police accountable, the generality of the statement was too much for Kelly. She noted that Nero had had no interaction with Gray on the day of his

The Kelly File

Kelly interviews Facebook COO and author Sheryl Sandberg.

In addition to addressing activists in the Black Lives Matter movement, Kelly took on a surprising number of contentious issues on *The Kelly File*. This, as noted earlier, broadened Fox's viewership substantially. While maintaining professional impartiality at all times, Kelly does not suffer fools. This made her program fun to watch as well as provocative. The live-format program began as a spinoff of *The O'Reilly Factor*. It focused on late-breaking stories. It also featured news analysis and in-depth investigative reports. Kelly's hard-hitting newsmaker interviews put it on the map.

On January 3, 2017, there was an announcement that Kelly would be leaving the network and moving to NBC News. The last episode of *The Kelly File* aired on January 6, marking Kelly's last day with Fox News.

arrest. She also pointed out the impossibility of locking up police for something so vague as bad judgment calls and the consequent danger to the community should that happen.

For Mckesson's part, he shot back (without interruption from Kelly) with a question: "Do you think Freddie Gray should be dead, Megyn? I will never agree that an officer's role is to kill unarmed citizens."[14] And there it rested. Rather than escalating an impossible argument, Kelly listened closely to Mckesson's words. She shared her own thoughts.

The end result was a peaceful exchange of ideas and opinions. Most of all, she realized that right and wrong could not be definitively located in so complex a story. In this way, Kelly helped subdue the fires of hatred and anger that threatened to prevail.

Working Mothers

Another cause that Kelly is passionate about is the plight of working mothers. Finding the balance between a career and motherhood is difficult at best. "We set the expectations too high for new mothers," Kelly maintains. "I'm always telling women, 'Don't expect to not hate it.' You're going to feel and look terrible, and you're going to wonder if you blew up your life. The cruel irony of it is, just at the time you're loving it and you've got it down, you have to go back to work."[15] This kind of practical advice has made Kelly someone who many women can relate to, and these women find her to be a role model for the audience of working mothers.

The mother of three shares an anecdote both harrowing and hilarious. A mere nine weeks after giving birth to son Thatcher, Kelly resumed anchoring her prime-time show, a decision which she now believes was too soon. At the same time, there was an appearance on *The Tonight Show* with Jay Leno during which both she and newborn Thatcher had a breakdown. "Five minutes before I had to go onstage, Thatcher was having a meltdown," Kelly recalls. "So I yank my dress open and start breastfeeding as I'm mic'd up."[16]

Whether the subject is workplace sexual harassment, Black Lives Matter, gay marriage and activism, religious persecution, or maternity leave, Kelly never hesitates to speak up and speak out, always with sharp intelligence, humor, and poise. These are the qualities that have distinguished her as an anchorwoman and have led her to become a strong leader in broadcast journalism.

CHAPTER SIX

Recognized and Honored

I n 2014, *Time* magazine honored Megyn Kelly as one its "100 Most Influential People." It's easy to see why the board of the august publication chose her. Prior to leaving Fox News, Kelly reached an estimated two million viewers nationwide. As a broadcast original, a reporter who defies the usual expectations, she has built up a legion of fans, a legion that transcends political divisions. As observed earlier, she never lets the needs of the status quo interfere with her integrity. She is her own woman, and it shows. Appropriately, *Time* placed her in its "Pioneers" section of influential people. Others in that category included a wide variety of inspiring trailblazers: maverick television writer Jenji Kohan; African missionary

Kelly attends the 2014 *Time* 100 Gala in New York City.

Sister Rosemary Nyirumbe; Jason Collins, the first openly gay, still active pro athlete in a major United States sports league; and intrepid Indian politician Arvind Kejriwal. None of them, like Kelly, are afraid to be catalysts for change in their quest to make the world a better place. They do this by excelling in their chosen professions, without compromising themselves. In his tribute to Kelly, good friend and mentor Brit Hume recalled, "From the start, Megyn gave us insightful Supreme Court coverage, and she was among the first to spot flaws in the false rape charges against the Duke lacrosse players. She was too good to last as a mere correspondent, and she didn't. The rest, as they say, is history."[1]

Her own response to the *Time* magazine honor was quintessentially Kelly: laughter and self-deprecation. By way of proof, she recalled a recent outing to the Broadway musical *The Bridges of Madison County* with her husband, Doug. After enjoying the show, the couple went backstage to greet the cast, led by veteran theater stars Steven Pasquale and Kelli O'Hara. When confronted with the famous face, they didn't recognize her, despite her recent *Time* honor and many years on Fox News.

Doing Unto Others

Kelly assists worthy causes of all kinds, often receiving recognition. She is especially concerned with abused children. This is no surprise. As a bullying and harassment survivor herself, she is keenly aware that she is not the only victim. She is on record as being disgusted by the statistics on child abuse in the United States. No wonder that the Childhelp agency, with its focus on helping abused and neglected youngsters, caught her eye. Based in Phoenix, Arizona, this agency has helped over ten million children through its programs of prevention, intervention, and treatment. Kelly got involved, and her work for them has been greatly appreciated. On April 6, 2011, National Hope Day, Kelly publicized this worthy charity on Fox News, using her on-air platform to solicit donations and provide critical information about the Childhelp phone number to a nationwide audience. That led to an especially meaningful accolade, when the show business bible, *Variety*, recognized her in its 2016 Power of Women: New York honors. Kelly does not take her authoritative voice for granted. She understands that it doesn't mean much unless it is put to good use by helping those in need.

Reaping the Rewards While Keeping the Balance

The broadcast world proved the ultimate fulfillment of Kelly's honest, hard work in college, law school, and the moot court. She had learned to trust in her inherent talents, in the alchemy between her outer beauty, inner integrity, and intellectual brilliance. *Vanity Fair* writer Evgenia Peretz describes her as "a woman of preternatural charisma … the alpha girl at the dinner party, the one telling the stories, cracking the jokes, the

Childhelp

"Every ten seconds in the country, someone calls up to report a child-abuse crime in progress," reports Megyn Kelly.[2] After receiving a 2009 award from the nonprofit Childhelp for covering these issues as an anchor on Fox News, she continued to stay involved by donating her time and appearing at fundraisers. Childhelp has since become the nation's largest nonprofit for abused youth, providing housing and counseling to victims, as well as a hotline with therapists available around the clock. Sara O'Meara, a founder of the charity, says Kelly has used her national profile to keep the spotlight on the work the organization does. "Megyn has helped us save a lot of children's lives," O'Meara says. "She is a doer as well as a talker."[3] Using her star power to shine a light on Childhelp has been a gratifying way for Kelly to give back.

one who is nice to everyone but leaves people wanting more."[4] Yet, however much her fame and popularity grew, her basic values, as honed early on by family and church, never wavered. She knew who she was.

Her *Time* recognition was well earned. It neatly contradicts the notion of what Kelly terms the "cupcake nation," that imaginary place where everyone is a winner. She frankly finds the concept dangerous as it fails to prepare children for the important experience of failure—of having to get up, dust yourself off, and try again. Strength and humility are the rewards of such challenges. One is deepened as a person. To be your true self is to be sometimes offended, hurt, or angry. That's OK. It's called growth. As Kelly says, "When we try to protect the young from any vaguely uncomfortable ideas or encounters, we do them a grave disservice. Being tested by different viewpoints in my life, being sometimes offended or occasionally hurt, or even targeted, is a big part of what prepared me for the challenges I've faced in my career."[5]

Indeed, Kelly's influence has spread far and wide, despite, until 2017, her exclusive **domicile** at Fox News. In the last few years, Kelly began questioning her role as a strictly Fox personality. Fox brought her into the limelight and made her a high-profile television star. They had asked for and received her entire loyalty. But it is important to remember that Fox also benefited tremendously from her work in terms of audience growth, ratings, and revenue. And there are other loyalties in life, especially loyalty to oneself. Kelly was too original a person to be typed as one kind of reporter, under the banner of one particular network. The time had come, she felt, to spread her wings at a different type of workplace. Having weathered the Trump and Ailes scandals, she looked at life in a new light. Kelly has said that "adversity is an opportunity."[6] Her trials and tribulations have strengthened her in ways she could not have imagined. It's one thing to have a tough exterior.

But without a compassionate, human interior, what is it worth? She began to evaluate her Fox position in a new way—grateful for the opportunities and success it had brought her, but unsure about how to go forward with it as the person she had become. As *Vanity Fair* writer Sarah Ellison said in a January 2017 profile, "One signal of her openness, a person close to Kelly told me, was that money, which once seemed insurmountable, would now be less of an issue. Kelly, it seemed, was ready to explore life outside the Fox News bunker."[7]

The use of the word "bunker" was an interesting choice to describe Fox News. "Bunker" is a military term that refers to a protective embankment or dugout, especially a fortified chamber mostly below ground and often built of reinforced concrete. In other words, a secret place in which to hide. For a woman looking to spread her wings and try new challenges, a "bunker" was the last place to be.

"Megyn Moments"

In 2016, when a variety of networks came courting, hoping to entice Kelly away from Fox, her mind was open. Briefly, this led to her becoming the story rather than reporting the story. The entire media was obsessed with Kelly and what her next move would be. Not everyone was rooting for her. The naysayers predicted she'd lose her popularity once she was no longer doing battle with Trump or Ailes. But others had a very different view. They looked forward to seeing what choice she would make. On January 3, 2017, Kelly herself announced on Twitter that she'd accepted an offer to move to NBC. "An ending and new beginning," as she succinctly put it.[8] Her departure from Fox was peaceful and accomplished without **rancor** or bad feeling. True to form, she left on a high note. Acting Fox News CEO, the media **mogul** Rupert Murdoch, released a kind statement, declaring, "We thank Megyn Kelly for her twelve years of contributions to Fox News. We hope she enjoys tremendous success in her career and wish her and her family all the best."[9]

Over at NBC, Kelly's new colleagues were genuinely excited at the prospect of her arrival. *Today* show host Matt Lauer, who celebrated his twentieth anniversary on the program in 2017, openly admires Kelly. "She's multitalented and would fit right in … She's a remarkable broadcaster and journalist, a real force," he said in an interview.[10] Perhaps NBC also had another accolade in mind, this one from Brit Hume. "Attractive-looking blond anchorwomen are not rare. Attractive-looking blond anchorwomen who speak with a fierce authority are rare. In fact, attractive looking anybody who speaks with that kind of authority are rare."[11]

Her achievements at Fox made her a hot prospect for livening things up at NBC. She gave Fox its biggest new hit in thirteen years with *The Kelly File*. Unpredictable and fiery, Kelly takes no prisoners. Doubtless, her new network will be in for its own share of "Megyn Moments," a phrase coined by *New York Times* reporter Jim Rutenberg. As discussed earlier, a "Megyn Moment," according to Rutenberg, is what happens when Kelly catches a guest off guard. She does this by listening patiently as he or she pursues a line of argument. Suddenly, Kelly isolates one part of the dialogue and terms it "nonsense." She often attacks the startled guest with his or her own words. Kelly's independent ideas and razor-sharp legal mind are always ready to pounce. *The Kelly File* was the scene of upsets for Republican stalwarts such as former vice president Dick Cheney. "Megyn Moments" continue to be very popular. They increased the rather limited Fox viewership and garnered an audience share usually reserved for the mainstream networks. In fact, compared to competitor Rachel Maddow on MSNBC, Kelly's audience of 2.8 million was four times larger. NBC is confident that she will bring that enthusiastic fan following with her.

The most famous "Megyn Moment" happened on election night 2012. By ten o'clock, Republican hopes for their presidential candidate, Mitt Romney, were fading. Along came Karl Rove, senior advisor and deputy chief of staff during the George W. Bush administration, to the Fox set, expressing certainty that Romney could still pull ahead. "Is this just math you do as a Republican to make yourself feel better? Or is it real?" Kelly snapped.[12] Amazingly, Rove refused to give in. The election was

Kelly gets ready for the 2012 Democratic National Convention.

declared for Obama at 11:30 when he won the crucial
swing state of Ohio. However, Rove disputed the call.
He started listing his own numbers from other precincts.
Laughing right at him, Kelly deadpanned, "That's
awkward."[13] Rove represented the portion of Fox's
audience for whom the thought of a second Obama
term was beyond belief. Fox chief Roger Ailes, watching
from home, quickly called the control room and ordered
producers to send Kelly to the network's "decision desk,"
where the analysts calling the election were working.
Taking the long walk from the anchor desk to the decision
desk on camera, Kelly was in complete command of the
moment. Smiling broadly, she acknowledged the stage
crew and other colleagues with a friendly wave. She was in

no hurry, her timing perfect. Upon reaching the decision desk, as *New York Times* writer Jim Rutenberg put it, she calmly "had the numbers crunchers tick through all the reasons Rove, who once called himself the keeper of 'the Math,' was wrong—totally, inexorably, hopelessly wrong."[14] It was a moment to go down in broadcast history.

Another triumphant "Megyn Moment" occurred in 2011. This was around the time Kelly's second child, Yardley, had been born. Conservative talk show host Mike Gallagher took this moment to deride Kelly for her maternity leave absence. Terming such leave "a racket" to avoid work, he put himself firmly behind the eight ball. In August, Kelly returned to Fox. She invited Gallagher to be a guest on her show. Regarding her maternity leave, she addressed him saying, "The United States is the only advanced country that doesn't require paid leave." She continued, "If anything, the United States is in the dark ages when it comes to maternity leave. And what is it about getting pregnant and carrying a baby nine months that you don't think deserves a few months off so bonding and recovery can take place? Hmm?"[15] When Gallagher asked if men could get the same time off, Kelly lowered the boom. "Guess what? Yes, they do. It's called the Family and Medical Leave Act," she said.[16] The moment did not go unnoticed. "Megyn Kelly Demolishes Mike Gallagher," a *Huffington Post* headline rejoiced. The left-leaning *Gawker* called it a "feminist triumph."[17]

Life Goes On

Kelly has always been a huge fan of Oprah Winfrey. Given the lessons of Kelly's youth, it's no wonder. Winfrey has never felt sorry for herself, never bemoaned her race or gender. She just got on with the job until she was so good that no one could ignore her. Kelly adopted this as a model early on. It certainly echoes her parents' theory of no rewards unless they are earned. She firmly believes that her success speaks for itself and has nothing to do with gender. Her husband, Douglas Brunt, puts it another way:

She's like a combination of Walter Cronkite, Barbara Walters, Oprah Winfrey, and then a Grisham character who's a scrappy guy from the other side of the tracks who has a rare gift for the law, in a Grace Kelly package, with a little Larry the Cable Guy sprinkled on top.[18]

It was a far different Megyn Kelly who left Fox News for NBC than the one who first started out at Fox in 2004. She was older and wiser, with an outstanding array of trophies and testimonials for her new office. Rather than being proudly displayed, they will probably collect dust while she gets to work.

Douglas Brunt

Douglas Brunt is Megyn Kelly's second husband, and if his name sounds familiar, that's because he's the writer of several bestselling thrillers, including his debut offering, *Ghosts of Manhattan*. An internet security executive turned author, he started dating Kelly at a decidedly rough time in her life, when the presence of a stalker had necessitated a round-the-clock security detail. Brunt was the CEO of Authentium, Inc., an internet security company, from 2001 until selling it in 2011. Previously, he'd been a consultant for the American management consulting firm Booz Allen Hamilton. Originally from Philadelphia, he attended the Haverford School before graduating from Duke University.

As for Kelly, she needed someone to lean on. It made for a good start. As their relationship grew deeper, each was hesitant and had concerns around commitment. These are two high-profile people, after all, who come with some intriguing baggage. Kelly's troubled situation provided a "war-time" thrill to the union, and when they found that they could survive in the trenches together, they decided to make it permanent. Their glamorous 2009 wedding was followed by the arrival of three children, all of whom live together on Manhattan's Upper West Side.

Kelly and second husband Douglas Brunt attend the annual Costume Institute Gala at the Metropolitan Museum of Art in New York City.

1992

She is awarded an undergraduate degree in political science from Syracuse University.

2004

Fox News hires Kelly.

2001

She marries Daniel Kendall, but they divorce in 2006.

Megyn Kelly is born in Champaign, Illinois, but the family soon moves to Syracuse, New York.

WJLA-TV hires Kelly as a general assignment reporter.

1970

2003

Kelly earns her law degree from Albany Law School. She becomes an associate in the Chicago office of the law firm Bickel and Brewer, followed by nine years as an associate at the Jones Day law firm.

Kelly marries Douglas Brunt.

2008

1995

2010

Kelly begins hosting her own two-hour afternoon show, *America Live*.

2013

Kelly leaves as host of *America Live* for maternity leave. She also debuts a new nightly program, *The Kelly File*, on Fox.

2016

Kelly's autobiography, *Settle for More*, is published.

Kelly serves as moderator of the first GOP presidential debate.

Kelly announces her move to NBC.

2017

2015

The presidential election night is covered by Kelly.

2012

SOURCE NOTES

Chapter 1

1. Howard Kurtz, "Why Megyn Kelly Is Leaving Fox News for NBC," Fox News, January 3, 2017, http://www.foxnews.com/entertainment/2017/01/03/why-megyn-kelly-is-leaving-fox-news-for-nbc.

2. Megyn Kelly, *Settle for More* (New York: HarperCollins, 2016), 26.

3. Ibid., 20.

4. Ibid., 33.

5. Ibid., 36.

6. Noreen Malone, "Megyn Kelly Can Save Fox News," *New Republic*, November 9, 2012, https://newrepublic.com/article/109941/megyn-kelly-can-save-fox-news.

7. Kelly, *Settle for More*, 38.

Chapter 2

1. Kelly, *Settle for More*, 43.

2. Chris Matyszczyk, "Megyn Kelly Accuses Shutterfly of Lying," CNET, December 24, 2016, https://www.cnet.com/news/megyn-kelly-accuses-shutterfly-of-lying.

3. Kelly, *Settle for More*, 61.

4. Rachel Stockman, "We Investigated Her Legal Background and Attorney Megyn Kelly's No 'Bimbo,'" LawNewz, January 28, 2016, http://lawnewz.com/high-profile/we-investigated-her-legal-background-and-attorney-megyn-kellys-no-bimbo.

5. Kelly, *Settle for More*, 76.

6. Ibid.

7. Ibid.

8. Ibid., 79.

Chapter 3

1. Kelly, *Settle for More*, 97.

2. Ibid., 108.

3. Evgenia Peretz, "Blowhards, Beware: Megyn Kelly Will Slay You Now," *Vanity Fair*, January 4, 2016, http://www.vanityfair.com/news/2015/12/megyn-kelly-fox-news-cover-story.

4. Kelly, *Settle for More*, 108.

5. Ibid., 107.

6. Ibid., 109.

7. Vanessa Friedman, "No One Tells Megyn Kelly What to Wear," *New York Times*, December 17, 2016, https://www.nytimes.com/2016/12/17/fashion/megyn-kelly-fox-fashion.html?_r=0.

8. Ibid.

Chapter 4

1. Kelly, *Settle for More*, 128.

2. Brit Hume, "The 100 Most Influential People: Megyn Kelly," *Time*, April 23, 2014, http://time.com/collection-post/70888/megyn-kelly-2014-time-100.

3. "Megyn Kelly and the Question that Changed Her Life Forever," CBS News, April 3, 2016, http://www.cbsnews.com/news/megyn-kelly-and-the-question-that-changed-her-life-forever.

4. Ibid.

Chapter 5

1. Kelly, *Settle for More*, 301.

2. Ibid., 304.

3. Esther Lee, "Megyn Kelly Has Had It with This Anti–Gay Marriage Activist: Watch Their Exchange," *Us Weekly*, January 8, 2016, http://www.usmagazine.com/celebrity-news/news/megyn-kelly-has-had-it-with-this-antigay-marriage-activist-watch-w161090.

4. Ibid.

5. "'You Want to Silence': Megyn Challenges CAIR Member Over Campaign Against Islam Critic," Fox News Insider, April 10, 2014, http://insider.foxnews.com/2014/04/10/you-want-silence-megyn-challenges-cair-member-over-campaign-against-islam-critic.

6. Jack Mirkinson, "Megyn Kelly to Keith Ablow: Chaz Bono Comments 'Adding to the Hate,'" *Huffington Post*, November 14, 2011, http://www.huffingtonpost.com/2011/09/14/megyn-kelly-keith-ablow-chaz-bono-dancing-stars_n_963020.html.

7. Peretz, "Blowhards Beware: Megyn Kelly Will Slay You Now."

8. Ibid.

9. Ibid.

10. Lindsey Bever and Abby Ohlheiser, "Baltimore Police: Freddie Gray Died from a 'Tragic Injury to His Spinal Cord," *Washington Post*, April 20, 2015, https://www.washingtonpost.com/news/morning-mix/wp/2015/04/20/baltimore-police-freddie-gray-arrested-without-force-or-incident-before-fatal-injury.

11. "Freddie Gray's Death in Police Custody—What We Know," BBC, May 23, 2016, http://www.bbc.com/news/world-us-canada-32400497.

12. Kevin Rector, "Charges Dropped, Freddie Gray Case Concludes with Zero Convictions Against Officers," *Baltimore Sun*, July 27, 2016, http://www.baltimoresun.com/news/maryland/freddie-gray/bs-md-ci-miller-pretrial-motions-20160727-story.html.

13. Daniel Reynolds, "Megyn Kelly and DeRay Mckesson Clash Over Freddie Gray," *Advocate*, May 24, 2016, http://www.

advocate.com/media/2016/5/24/megyn-kelly-and-deray-mckesson-clash-over-freddie-gray.

14. Ibid.

15. Mehera Bonner, "Megyn Kelly Thinks We Set Expectations Too High for New Mothers," *Marie Claire*, March 17, 2016, http://www.marieclaire.com/celebrity/news/a19372/megyn-kelly-motherhood.

16. Ibid.

Chapter 6

1. Brit Hume, "The 100 Most Influential People."

2. Ramin Setoodeh, "Megyn Kelly Shines a Light on Child Abuse Nonprofit," *Variety*, April 5, 2016, http://variety.com/2016/tv/news/megyn-kelly-childhelp-abuse-1201745257.

3. Ibid.

4. Peretz, "Blowhards Beware: Megyn Kelly Will Slay You Now."

5. Erik Wemple, "Megyn Kelly: 'Fox Was Not Without Sin' in 2016 Campaign Coverage," *Washington Post*, December 19, 2016, https://www.washingtonpost.com/blogs/erik-wemple/wp/2016/12/19/megyn-kelly-fox-was-not-without-sin-in-2016-campaign-coverage.

6. Aurelie Corinthios, "Megyn Kelly Believes President Donald Trump Could Be 'Dangerous,'" *People*, November 16, 2016, http://people.com/politics/megyn-kelly-believes-president-donald-trump-could-be-dangerous.

7. Sarah Ellison, "Inside the Megyn Kelly–Fox News Split," *Vanity Fair*, January 3, 2017, http://www.vanityfair.com/news/2017/01/inside-the-megyn-kelly-fox-news-split.

8. Rachel Dicker, "Megyn Kelly Leaving Fox News for NBC," *US News & World Report*, January 3, 2017, https://www.usnews.com/news/national-news/articles/2017-01-03/megyn-kelly-leaving-fox-news-for-nbc.

9. Jim Rutenberg, "Megyn Kelly's Jump to NBC from Fox News Will Test Her, and the Networks," *New York Times*,

January 3, 2017, https://www.nytimes.com/2017/01/03/business/media/megyn-kelly-nbc-fox-news.html?_r=0.

10. Dana Rose Falcone, "Matt Lauer: Katie Couric Is Sort of My 'Soul Mate,'" *Us Weekly*, February 17, 2017, http://www.usmagazine.com/celebrity-news/news/matt-lauer-katie-couric-is-sort-of-my-soul-mate-w467665.

11. Luke Brinker, "Brit Hume Grossly Marvels that Megyn Kelly is Both Smart and Attractive," *Salon*, January 21, 2015, http://www.salon.com/2015/01/21/brit_hume_grossly_marvels_that_megyn_kelly_is_both_smart_and_attractive.

12. Kelly, *Settle for More*, 190.

13. Ibid.

14. Jim Rutenberg, "The Megyn Kelly Moment," *New York Times*, January 21, 2015, https://www.nytimes.com/2015/01/25/magazine/the-megyn-kelly-moment.html.

15. Ibid.

16. Kelly, *Settle for More*, 184.

17. Rutenberg, "The Megyn Kelly Moment."

18. Peretz, "Blowhards Beware: Megyn Kelly Will Slay You Now."

GLOSSARY

appellate In the law, having the power or authority to review, and possibly overturn, the decisions of another court.

bromide A commonplace statement or notion that suggests lack of sincerity in the speaker.

cause célèbre A notorious person, thing, incident, or episode that attracts a great deal of attention. The term comes from the French language, and it literally translates to the phrase "celebrated case."

depression A long slump in the economy. In the United States, the Great Depression began soon after the stock market crash of October 1929, which sent Wall Street into a panic and wiped out millions of investors.

domicile The place that a person identifies as a permanent home because of a strong connection to the place.

due diligence Due diligence refers to the act of doing research with care and responsibility.

federal prosecutor A federal prosecutor represents the United States federal government in United States district courts and United States courts of appeals. The prosecutor is the legal party responsible for presenting the case against an individual suspected of breaking the law.

gravitas A Latin word meaning high seriousness, dignity, or solemnity (as in a person's bearing or in the treatment of a subject).

idiosyncrasies Peculiarities or distinctive qualities of constitution or temperament.

incendiary Highly controversial; likely to provoke strong reactions or arguments.

innuendo An implied meaning or a veiled reflection on character or reputation.

jurisdictional rules Jurisdictional rules limit the power and authority of the courts.

mogul A powerful or significant person in a particular industry, usually media.

nuances A nuance is a subtle difference in or shade of meaning, expression, or sound.

probity Integrity and honesty; the quality of having a strong sense of morals.

rancor Bitterness or resentment, especially when those feelings last for a long time.

raucous Harsh or shrill.

rhetoric The art of effective or persuasive speaking or writing, especially through the use of figures of speech and other compositional techniques.

stalwart Loyal or committed.

status quo The general existing state of affairs, or the way things are; the current situation.

FURTHER INFORMATION

Books

Brock, David, Ari Rabin-Havt, and Media Matters for America. *The Fox Effect: How Roger Ailes Turned a Network into a Propaganda Machine*. New York: Anchor Books, 2012.

Perino, Dana. *And the Good News Is … Lessons and Advice from the Bright Side*. New York: Hachette Book Group, Inc., 2015.

Sherman, Gabriel. *The Loudest Voice in the Room: How the Brilliant, Bombastic Roger Ailes Built Fox News—and Divided a Country*. New York: Random House, 2014.

Websites

Becoming a Reporter—Career Girls
https://www.careergirls.org/resources/how-do-i-do-this/reporter

Aspiring news journalists will value this vast information resource that connects them to all aspects of a news journalism career.

Childhelp
https://www.childhelp.org

Childhelp is a nonprofit charity, and the Childhelp website provides detailed information on the prevention and treatment of child abuse.

Fox News
http://www.FoxNews.com

This website contains breaking news, entertainment features, health articles, and more.

NBC Television Network
http://www.nbc.com

This official website for the National Broadcasting Corporation provides detailed programming information, videos, and schedules.

Working Mother
http://www.workingmother.com

Working Mother is a lively news center that includes direct links for issues pertaining to women who work and have children.

Video

Megyn Kelly's Interview with Donald Trump
https://www.youtube.com/watch?v=UGPvwdrlzCM

Megyn Kelly interviews Donald Trump and questions his campaign style.

BIBLIOGRAPHY

Borchers, Callum. "Sorry, Donald Trump. But Megyn Kelly Is a Fantastic Debate Moderator." *Washington Post*, January 29, 2016. https://www.washingtonpost.com/news/the-fix/wp/2016/01/29/megyn-kelly-is-a-very-good-debate-moderator-heres-proof.

Dicker, Rachel. "Megyn Kelly Leaving Fox News For NBC." *US News & World Report*, January 3, 2017. https://www.usnews.com/news/national-news/articles/2017-01-03/megyn-kelly-leaving-fox-news-for-nbc.

Ellis, Lindsay. "Megyn Kelly of Fox News Honored at Bethlehem Central High School." *Times Union*, September 26, 2015. http://www.timesunion.com/local/article/Megyn-Kelly-of-Fox-News-honored-at-Bethlehem-6532483.php.

Ellison, Sarah. "Inside the Megyn Kelly–Fox News Split." *Vanity Fair*, January 3, 2017. http://www.vanityfair.com/news/2017/01/inside-the-megyn-kelly-fox-news-split.

Falcone, Dana Rose. "Matt Lauer: Katie Couric Is Sort of My 'Soul Mate.'" *Us Weekly*, February 17, 2017. http://www.usmagazine.com/celebrity-news/news/matt-lauer-katie-couric-is-sort-of-my-soul-mate-w467665.

Flanagan, Caitlin. "Can Megyn Kelly Escape Her Past?" *Atlantic*, March 2017. https://www.theatlantic.com/magazine/archive/2017/03/can-megyn-kelly-escape-her-past/513842.

Friedman, Jonah. "Megyn's Moment Will Prove Fleeting," *American Spectator*, January 5, 2017. https://spectator.org/megyns-moment-will-prove-fleeting.

Friedman, Vanessa. "No One Tells Megyn Kelly What to Wear." *New York Times*, December 17, 2016. https://www.nytimes. com/2016/12/17/fashion/megyn-kelly-fox-fashion.html.

Grynbaum, Michael M., and John Koblin. "Anchor Becomes News as Megyn Kelly Leaves Fox News for NBC," *New York Times*, January 3, 2017. https://www.nytimes. com/2017/01/03/business/media/megyn-kelly-leaves-fox-news-for-nbc.html.

Guthrie, Marisa. "Megyn Kelly Gets Candid: 'Dangerous' Roger Ailes, Her Trump Saga, That Offer, and Why She Won't Call Herself a Feminist." *Hollywood Reporter*, November 16, 2016. http://www.hollywoodreporter.com/features/megyn-kelly-gets-candid-dangerous-roger-ailes-her-trump-saga-offer-why-she-wont-call-a-femi.

Haller, Scot. "The Two Faces of a Newswoman." *People*, November 7, 1983. http://people.com/archive/cover-story-the-two-faces-of-a-newswoman-vol-20-no-19.

Horton, Helena. "Megyn Kelly Leaves Fox News: Here's a Round-Up of Her Best Bust-Ups with Donald Trump." *Telegraph*, January 3, 2017. http://www.telegraph.co.uk/news/2017/01/03/megyn-kelly-reportedly-leaves-fox-news-round-up-best-bust-ups.

Hume, Brit. "The 100 Most Influential People: Megyn Kelly." *Time*, April 23, 2014. http://time.com/collection-post/70888/megyn-kelly-2014-time-100.

"Interview: Megyn Kelly Reacts to Making the 'Time 100.'" Fox News Insider, April 24, 2014. http://insider.foxnews. com/2014/04/24/interview-megyn-kelly-reacts-fox-friends-after-being-named-times-100-most-influential.

Kelly, Megyn. *Settle for More*. New York: HarperCollins, 2016.

Kurtz, Howard. "Why Megyn Kelly Is Leaving Fox News for NBC." Fox News, January 3, 2017. http://www.foxnews.com/

entertainment/2017/01/03/why-megyn-kelly-is-leaving-fox-news-for-nbc.html.

Lee, Esther. "Megyn Kelly Has Had It with This Anti–Gay Marriage Activist: Watch Their Exchange." *Us Weekly*, January 8, 2016. http://www.usmagazine.com/celebrity-news/news/megyn-kelly-has-had-it-with-this-antigay-marriage-activist-watch-w161090.

"Megyn Kelly and the Question That Changed Her Life Forever." CBS News, April 3, 2016. http://www.cbsnews.com/news/megyn-kelly-and-the-question-that-changed-her-life-forever/2.

Mizoguchi, Karen. "Megyn Kelly: 'We Set the Expectations Too High for New Mothers.'" *People*, March 16, 2016. http://celebritybabies.people.com/2016/03/16/megyn-kelly-more-we-set-the-expectations-too-high-for-new-mothers.

"Moot Court Program." Syracuse University College of Law. Accessed March 25, 2017. http://law.syr.edu/academics/advocacy-program/moot-court-program.

O'Connor, Maureen. "Megyn Kelly Destroys Guy Who Called Her Maternity Leave 'a Racket.'" *Gawker*, August 8, 2011. http://gawker.com/5828842/megyn-kelly-destroys-guy-who-called-her-maternity-leave-a-racket.

O'Shea, Chris. "Megyn Kelly Covers Vanity Fair." *Adweek*, January 4, 2016. http://www.adweek.com/digital/megyn-kelly-covers-vanity-fair-707515.

Peretz, Evgenia. "Blowhards Beware: Megyn Kelly Will Slay You Now." *Vanity Fair*, January 4, 2016. http://www.vanityfair.com/news/2015/12/megyn-kelly-fox-news-cover-story.

Rector, Kevin. "Charges Dropped, Freddie Gray Case Concludes with Zero Convictions Against Officers." *Baltimore Sun*, July 27, 2016. http://www.baltimoresun.com/news/maryland/freddie-gray/bs-md-ci-miller-pretrial-motions-20160727-story.html.

Reynolds, Daniel. "Megyn Kelly and DeRay Mckesson Clash Over Freddie Gray." *Advocate*, May 24, 2016. http://www. advocate.com/media/2016/5/24/megyn-kelly-and-deray-mckesson-clash-over-freddie-gray.

Robinson, Judah. "Watch This Anti-Gay Activist Try to Explain the Supreme Court to Megyn Kelly." *Huffington Post*, January 7, 2016. http://www.huffingtonpost.com/entry/brian-brown-gay-marriage-megyn-kelly_us_568e9d72e4b0a2b6fb6f0978.

Rudolph, Ileane. "Matt Lauer Opens Up About 20 Years at 'Today,' His Cohosts, and New Coworker Megyn Kelly." *TV Insider*, February 9, 2017. https://www.tvinsider. com/115246/matt-lauer-today-twentieth-anniversary.

Rutenberg, Jim. "The Megyn Kelly Moment." *New York Times*, January 21, 2015. https://www.nytimes.com/2015/01/25/ magazine/the-megyn-kelly-moment.html?_r=0.

Setoodeh, Ramin. "Megyn Kelly Shines a Light on Child Abuse Nonprofit." *Variety*, April 5, 2016. https://www. variety.com/2016/tv/news/megyn-kelly-childhelp-abuse-1201745257.

Shaw, Lucas. "Fox News Retooled Lineup Draws Highest Ratings Since Iraq." Bloomberg Technology, September 30, 2014. https://www.bloomberg.com/news/ articles/2014-09-30/fox-news-retooled-lineup-draws-highest-ratings-since-iraq.

Sherman, Gabriel. "The Revenge of Roger's Angels: How Fox News Women Took Down the Most Powerful, and Predatory, Man in Media." *New York Magazine*, September 2, 2016. http://nymag.com/daily/intelligencer/2016/09/how-fox-news-women-took-down-roger-ailes.html.

Silman, Anna. "What Should Feminists Make of Megyn Kelly?" *New York Magazine*, November 18, 2016. http://nymag.com/ thecut/2016/11/what-should-feminists-make-of-megyn-kelly.html.

Stockman, Rachel. "We Investigated Her Legal Background and Megyn Kelly's No 'Bimbo.'" LawNewz, January 28, 2016. http://lawnewz.com/high-profile/we-investigated-her-legal-background-and-attorney-megyn-kellys-no-bimbo.

Thomas, Lowell Jackson. *So Long Until Tomorrow*: *From Quaker Hill to Kathmandu*. New York: William Morrow, 1977.

Wagner, Laura. "Megyn Kelly Is Leaving Fox News to Join NBC News." NPR, January 3, 2017. http://www.npr.org/sections/thetwo-way/2017/01/03/508046088/megyn-kelly-is-leaving-fox-news-to-join-nbc-news.

INDEX

Page numbers in **boldface** are illustrations. Entries in **boldface** are glossary terms.

ABOUT THE AUTHOR

Phoebe Collins has published articles on travel and the arts in *Aishti*, *Ambassador Media*, *Dog Fancy*, and *Cinematheque*. She has been a contributing writer and editor on many books and worked as an acquisitions editor. Upstate New York is home, where she enjoys theater, concerts, and outdoor activities.

DISCARD

APR - - 2018

Wakarusa Public Library